Praise for

perfectly imperfect

"Baron says exactly what our spirits need to hear. *Perfectly Imperfect* is the real deal! It's honest, insightful, and inspiring, and it shows us the true meaning and power of yoga. This book will wake up every aspect of your practice and give you the tools you need to show up fully every day, both on and off the mat. This is a seriously empowering read."

— Gabrielle Bernstein, *New York Times* best-selling author of *Miracles Now*

perfectly imperfect

ALSO BY BARON BAPTISTE

Books

*BEING OF POWER: The 9 Practices to
Ignite an Empowered Life**

*40 DAYS TO PERSONAL REVOLUTION: A Breakthrough
Program to Radically Change Your Body and
Awaken the Sacred Within Your Soul*

*JOURNEY INTO POWER: How to Sculpt Your Ideal Body,
Free Your True Self, and Transform Your Life with Yoga*

MY DADDY IS A PRETZEL: Yoga for Parents and Kids

*THE YOGA BOOTCAMP BOX: An Interactive
Program to Revolutionize Your Life with Yoga*

CDs and DVDs

BAPTISTE LIVE

ENERGIZE AND ELEVATE with Baron Baptiste

IGNITE & INTEGRATE with Baron Baptiste

JOURNEY INTO POWER: Power Vinyasa Yoga, Level 1

JOURNEY INTO POWER: Power Vinyasa Yoga, Level 2

MEDITATION FOR BEGINNERS

*Available from Hay House
Please visit:

Hay House USA: www.hayhouse.com®
Hay House Australia: www.hayhouse.com.au
Hay House UK: www.hayhouse.co.uk
Hay House India: www.hayhouse.co.in

perfectly imperfect

THE ART AND SOUL OF
YOGA PRACTICE

BARON BAPTISTE

HAY HOUSE INDIA
Australia • Canada • Hong Kong • India
South Africa • United Kingdom • United States

Hay House Publishers (India) Pvt. Ltd.
Muskaan Complex, Plot No.3, B-2 Vasant Kunj, New Delhi-110 070, India
Hay House Inc., PO Box 5100, Carlsbad, CA 92018-5100, USA
Hay House UK, Ltd., Astley House, 33 Notting Hill Gate, London W11 3JQ, UK
Hay House Australia Pty Ltd., 18/36 Ralph St., Alexandria NSW 2015, Australia
Hay House SA (Pty) Ltd., PO Box 990, Witkoppen 2068, South Africa
Hay House Publishing, Ltd., 17/F, One Hysan Ave., Causeway Bay, Hong Kong
Raincoast, 9050 Shaughnessy St., Vancouver, BC V6P 6E5, Canada
www.hayhouse.co.in
email: contact@hayhouse.co.in

First Indian edition 2016

The author of this book does not dispense medical advice or prescribe the use
of any technique as a form of treatment for physical or medical problems
without the advice of a physician, either directly or indirectly. The intent
of the author is only to offer information of a general nature to help you
in your quest for emotional and spiritual well-being. In the event you use
any of the information in this book for yourself, which is your constitutional
right, the author and the publisher assume no responsibility for your actions.

FOR SALE IN THE INDIAN SUBCONTINENT ONLY

ISBN 978-93-85827-14-3

Printed and bound at
Rajkamal Electric Press, Sonipat, Haryana, India

contents

introduction

I've spent my whole life either surrounded by or practicing yoga. From the time I was a young boy, it was as much a part of my life as school, or baseball, or surfing at the beach with my friends. I grew up in San Francisco, where my parents opened one of the first yoga schools and natural health centers in the United States. If they weren't practicing yoga, they were teaching it, or hosting one of the many well-known yoga masters who came over from India to stay as guests in our home.

I had the privilege of studying directly under some of the world's greatest teachers. In time, I grew into an accomplished yoga practitioner and teacher in my own right, very adept at looking and sounding like a "real yogi." I could recite the Yoga Sutras, call out any pose in Sanskrit, balance as still as a statue, and bend my body into the fanciest of poses.

And yet, something was missing. I was strong. I was supple. I looked healthy. I was in great shape. But there was a greater sense of meaning and purpose lacking in what I was doing. Somehow it all felt like I was just going through the motions. Which, it turns out, I was. What was missing in my practice and in my teaching was power. Not power over others—which is how we typically define power—but a power that was generated from within. I woke up and saw that I needed to access a new kind of power to elevate not just my practice on the mat, but my entire life.

After that realization, my whole life opened up. I went through many transformations, breakdowns, and breakthroughs. I discovered my authentic voice and began to teach not through the filter of rote knowledge but from my own authentic process of inquiry and discovery. All of this led to the development of the methodology I teach today.

I've written five books, taught hundreds of thousands of yoga enthusiasts, and trained thousands of yoga teachers all around the world. Through it all, what matters most to me is that they—and you—are awakened to their own sense of power and possibility and their ability to apply it, live it, and be it in all things on the mat and off. So in this book, I offer you a look into my classroom and share the essential lessons and insights I have excavated and cultivated from my teaching and coaching experiences with real people dealing with real life.

Applying the proper form and alignment of yoga poses is, of course, important, but this book is about what goes on for you *after* you take the pose—in what I call the *receiving pose*. What goes through your mind? What stops you or inspires you? What tools can you use to empower your poses and your practice right now? What if you completely altered how the pose occurs for you, and through the pose were able to transform how life shows up for you?

The mystery and challenge of yoga is that much is discovered through a rigorous physical practice, yet its greatest power lies beyond the realm of the body. Yes, at its most basic, yoga is a series of physical poses, but a practice aimed solely at physical thresholds is limiting. You might be strong, or flexible, or able to stick a beautiful handstand in the middle of the room, and that's fulfilling and impressive on one level, but ultimately, so what? I love the feeling of being strong and in shape as much as anyone else. But as I've learned, it's incomplete. Having a masterful yoga practice is about creating a whole new paradigm for yourself as a human being—not just a human body. The work you do on the mat facilitates your whole life. When you transform on your mat, you transform your vitality and your viewpoint. It's the same you, in the same body, against the same landscape of life, only you have a new vantage point. As you transform yourself as the seer, everything about how you show up in the world—and how the world shows up for you—is altered.

The ultimate goal for any yogi is to make the highest call at each step. We do this by creating what I call *true north alignment*—the state of holistic integration in which your body, mind, breath, and life energy are wholly united and aimed into your greater purpose, much like a compass pointing in the right direction. In true north alignment, you access your innate wisdom to know when to dig deeper and ask more of yourself, or when to practice the art of "let it be." You dance with what is and face what's coming up for you in this very moment, and wake up to what's possible. And, when you discover your attention and energy has drifted away from your true north, you simply bring yourself back and begin again, as often as you need to. This is what it means to have a powerful, life-transforming practice.

My path and process have been perfectly imperfect. As I have strived to do the work on the mat and messily brought it off the mat into all the other areas of my life, I see now that it has all happened perfectly, even though it looked quite the opposite. I have come to see that everything I once considered a missed opportunity, wrong turn, or mistake along the way is actually as much a part of my path as the successes and triumphs. I can now look back and see that yoga practice has been the unifier—the true north practice that has aligned my body, my being, and my life direction. From my true north, I have a place to stand as I—along with many other empowered Baptiste Yoga teachers—carry the spirit, message, and methodology of Baptiste Yoga to empower physical health, mental composure, and emotional well-being to many other people around the world.

With this book, my aim is to support you in your own discovery of all that and more. The transformative power of any knowledge is in discovering it for yourself, through your own experience. The foundational pieces in this book will shine new light on your journey, ignite your practice with new power, inspire new possibilities for growth, and infuse your life with the grace and confidence you seek.

Baron Baptiste
June, 2015

why do yoga?

All learning is remembering.

PLATO

I'm at the Baptiste Power Yoga Institute in Boston, lying on my back in Savasana. I've just completed an amazing power vinyasa yoga practice and I'm drenched in sweat; it's pouring off my body and into my eyes. My heart is pounding in my chest. I'm flush with a mix of exhilaration, release, and gratitude.

I'm grateful to have just experienced a rigorous and inspiring yoga practice led by a certified Baptiste Yoga teacher named Gregor Singleton. Gregor has been a part of my teaching team for many years, so I already knew he was a strong teacher whose classes deliver a potent experience, but in this moment, I was overtaken with a sense of profound appreciation. I was deeply moved to have a practice that I've sourced and developed over many years be reflected back to me so powerfully by another human being. I'd always dreamed of being a leader who develops other leaders so they can make a contribution to humanity and community, one pose at a time. Here I was today, lying in Savasana, literally experiencing my dream come true.

As I lay there, I reflected back to what the practice has given me from my early days when I was newer to the practice all the way up until this moment. In my youth, I would often surf underneath the Golden Gate Bridge in San Francisco. Sometimes the fog would move in and completely obscure the bridge, making it appear as if the bridge did not exist at all. Then the wind would pick up and blow the fog away, and suddenly the enormous beautiful Golden Gate Bridge would re-appear.

That's exactly how the practice of yoga has worked for me. Whenever I get lost in a personal fog and have the experience of losing myself and my inner true north, the practice has been like a cleansing windstorm that would dissipate the fog and reveal the inner knowing that's inherently there within me, re-grounding me in what's true. I like to call this experience *trueing up*.

You already know what you need in order to live an extraordinary life that you love. That knowledge is within you. Perhaps obscured, but it is still there. Many a time on my mat, or in meditation, I've been hit with a recurring revelation that seemed to whisper into my ear, "Baron, allow yourself to know that you already know what you need to know." Whenever I would take my confidence from that inner knowing and revelation, the entire quality of my life would inevitably be enhanced.

In many ways, yoga is a practice not of building, but of uncovering. It is the ultimate excavation tool for the soul.

At a certain point in the early days of my practice, I realized that I lived my life in a box. As someone who was committed to success and growth, I would persistently explore the opportunities and various pathways to better myself and my life, but only within the limits of that box. I would even explore the different outer edges and the corners of the box, but still I was limited to what's available inside the one box I called *my life as I know it.*

What the practice gave me is the ability to create new alternative boxes for my life rather than being limited to just doing more of the same things inside the limits of the same box, or doing the same things better or differently—which is really just improving things inside the same box. I realized that yoga practice is about creating new boxes for yourself that contain as-yet-unseen possibilities for elevating the quality of your life.

Outside our usual box of "life as we know it," we see and hear differently. One of the most powerful skills I began to develop when I stepped outside the box of my own created reality (i.e., "my life as I know it") was the ability to listen and truly notice the details of the world around me. I began to observe people close to me and the people I worked with through new eyes and ears, as if I were watching a film. I began to observe their bodies and movements and the ways they engage in conversations, cook, work, walk, sit. I started to really see how they moved on their mat through poses.

And I also began to observe myself. I saw that typically people bring themselves to yoga to get fixed . . . to get rid of their problems . . . to get happy. And I saw that I was one of those people, too.

Back then, I had an almost superstitious belief that yoga was the ultimate fixer. By all appearances, my life and asana practice looked pretty good, but way down deep I had a fundamental belief that I wasn't okay.

I felt there was something wrong with me, and this disempowering belief was the lens through which I viewed all of life. Skillful at wearing masks, I hid this deep, dark, dirty truth about myself from everyone.

Being a "seeker of growth" seemed like a positive characteristic to have, so I threw myself into my yoga practice and studies. I now know that traveling my spiritual path was a sophisticated way to cover up the feeling that I was broken. I kept seeking, believing if I found the right guru and the right yoga teachings, all would get fixed within me and all my problems would disappear.

After several thousands of hours on the mat, and years of daily meditation, I reached a surprising and important personal revelation: no one *needs* yoga. Including me.

The only things you and I need to physically survive as human beings are air to breathe, water to drink, food to eat, and shelter from the elements. To function emotionally, we need someone to love and someone to love us. Spiritually, we need to feel some sense of self-respect and the admiration of others. When these basic human needs aren't filled, we don't do well. Any human being can meet these needs without ever doing a yoga pose.

This insight was huge for me, and it started an inquiry of "Why do yoga?" Really, I wanted to know: What was available from this ancient practice beyond the obvious physical benefits?

I realized that the deeper aim of the practice is not to solve problems and that there is, in fact, nothing to fix. Although many of us have had the experience of having some of our issues dissolve in the heat and flow of moving through poses, the point of the practice is not so yogis can work on or get rid of their problems.

When I went beyond the physical emphasis of the practice, it became about those exceptional and rare times in life when I had the experience of being absolutely whole, complete, and at perfect peace with myself and my surroundings. I don't mean the kind of gratification we experience when accomplishing a goal or attaining something we desire. I am speaking to the experience of being absolutely aligned in oneself, with nothing being "wrong" about what is exactly as it is, and nothing lacking. This is true north alignment.

Each of us has experienced moments of true north alignment in our lives: those moments when we are fully alive in body and being, connected to all of life. In such true north moments you experience that the pose, and all of life, is perfect exactly as it is. In such moments we have no urge for the pose to be different, or better. There is no lack. There is no sense of disappointment or comparison to what should or should not be, no sense that the pose is not what we worked for. In these moments we feel open, undefended with no need to protect. There is no urge to hold on, consume, or collect. We are aligned with and flowing from our greater purpose. Such moments are perfect as they are, for however long they may last.

As I stayed in the inquiry of "Why do yoga?," I saw that people function successfully in life without such moments, too. Like the practice of yoga, such moments are not necessities. They aren't something we "should" have or do, and they aren't necessarily even "good for us," like taking vitamins or exercising. They do not make us any better or smarter or sexier or more successful than anyone else. These true north moments—these experiences of being perfectly whole—are sufficient unto themselves.

Beyond the physical benefits, and even beyond the true north alignment moments, one finds something else in yoga: the opportunity to discover that space within yourself where such moments originate—actually where you and life originate. You shift from being a character in the story of life to being the playwright authoring the story creatively, consciously, freely, and totally. In an even broader sense, you become the space in which the whole story of your life occurs.

the dance of
yes and no

The oldest, shortest words—"yes" and "no"—are those which require the most thought.

PYTHAGORAS

There are only two ways we show up on our mat and in life: as a *yes*, or as a *no*. *Yes* carries the energy of possibility; *no* carries the energy of resistance. *Yes* expresses your willingness to claim your power and use it to discover the real meaning of commitment. *Yes* invites you to expand and to come into your full creative expression. It opens you up and affirms your willingness to be teachable when you don't have the know-how to get where you want to go. *Yes* affirms the existence of a destination in the practice beyond mere physical gain.

No shows up with very different energy. It is closed, rigid, and often stubborn. It takes the form of excuses, complaints, procrastination, resistance, frustration, and so on. *No* impedes, or flat-out stops you in your tracks.

You are always in a dance of *yes* and *no*. Being a *yes* for anything automatically makes you a *no* for something else. In fact, if we cannot point to what we are saying *no* to, then our *yes* means nothing. If you are a *yes* for peace, you are a *no* for war. If you are a *yes* for creating vibrancy and health in your body, you are a *no* for ingesting junk food, doing drugs, and so on. If you are a *yes* for full acceptance in your relationship, you are a *no* for criticizing and trying to change the person you love. If you are a *yes* for growth, you are a *no* for procrastination and stagnation.

Looking at this from the other side of the lens, we see that saying *no* is the action of saying *yes* to something else. In my younger days I was a *no* for yoga. I would not have it, would not practice it; my *yes* was for defying everything my father wanted me to do. In my youth, my consequence for any misbehaving or poor grades at school was that I would have to attend my parents' yoga classes, the one thing I resisted most. While in their classes, I mostly couldn't wait for every pose and every part of the class to be over. I would count the breaths and the minutes, willing time to move faster. Being a *no* for yoga bound me to time while in the practice and locked in a steady mantra of "Is this over yet?"

I've since come to learn that in contrast to *no, yes* allows for a sense of timelessness and the joy of being fully in my experience. In my early twenties, while on a meditation and yoga retreat at my parents' retreat center on the beach in Central America, I experienced the unique and profound result of the practice. I felt a strong, energetic warmth emerge up from my solar plexus and take me into a state of feeling completely carefree, safe, and wholly awake and aware. That fundamental shift in my being altered my life forever. It was like I really got the practice in body and being. From that moment, saying *yes* to the practice was a natural expression for me.

I share this with you to invite you to engage in your own inquiry of "What am I a *yes* for in my practice?" and "What do I refuse and say *no* to?" Or, to put it another way, "How am I showing up on my mat and in my life?"

•

Yes and *no* take the form of emotional energy, and emotions contain vibrations. That sounds esoteric, I know, but in your body and your being, you can feel it as something tangible. Think about when you're around someone who is angry; you can feel that vibration of rage, can't you? Similarly, someone who is happy gives off a different kind of vibration, radiating a sense of lightness and joy. These different vibrations of *yes* and *no* have an impact on your body, and on your energetic capacity to support or block what you're up to in the pose and in your life.

Emotional vibrations fuel our actions. In other words, being a *yes* or being a *no* will dictate what you do or don't do. Consider that when you are inspired by the possibility of something, your body vibrates at the perfect frequency to support you in achieving the thing that inspires you. The energetic vibration of *yes* carries the emotional energy of enthusiasm, which translates into action. You are naturally moved and inspired to create and achieve.

An important personal discovery for me was when I got clear that the only way I could impact my practice was through action. The pose does not care what I intend, how committed I am, how I feel, or what I think, and it certainly has no interest in what I like and don't like. Take a look and see for yourself that poses only really evolve for you when you act into what you want to create. When you are a *yes* for what's possible in your practice, you will act. And out of that action, you will expand and create a new physical reality.

My 15-year-old son, Malachi, participated in a Level One teacher training I led in Arizona. After the training, he was all lit up about what was possible in his yoga practice. On our first day home, he said to me, "Dad, I haven't tried it yet, but do you think I could press from Crow Pose into handstand?" I responded, "Be a *yes* for it and see what happens."

Malachi smiled, set his hands on the floor right in the middle of our living room, and took Crow Pose . . . then pressed straight up into handstand! He didn't ask how to do it; he asked, "Can I do it?" and the answer was a resounding YES. Regardless of whether he was able to achieve handstand from Crow Pose or not, he empowered himself to be a participating player instead of a spectator to his own experience.

You may want to rise up into handstand from crow, or silently jump forward from Chaturanga, and that desire is great. It matters. But it is only half the game. The other half is being a YES—fully, wholly, and honestly—for what you are aiming for. To aim true in the pose is to be a *yes* for the results you want. It's not magic. You won't rise up into a perfect handstand simply through embodying the energy of *yes*, but you will find that being a *yes* inspires you to take the actions needed to move from where you are to where you want to go.

Those who fall into the trap of people pleasing tend to say *yes* when they really want to say *no*. In the practice of yoga asana, we can try authentically saying *yes* to what we want. I call this *aiming true*. Carl Jung said that all consciousness begins with an act of disobedience. Our dignity is found in our ability to say *no* to the things we don't want—to disobey the urge to say *yes* when we really want to say *no*—and open the door to saying *yes* to pursuing our true desires.

Today, on your mat, are you a *yes* for deep, rhythmic breath (called *ujjayi*), or a *no*? If you are a *yes*, it will enable your breath to carry you with ease. Are you a *yes* for a fixed, steady gaze (*drishti*) or a *no*? If you are a *yes*, it will give you the action of focusing your gaze with intent and fire. Are you a *yes* for lightness and play on your mat, or a *no*? If you are a *yes*, your practice will be buoyed by joy.

It's important to know where your inner compass is pointing; this is how you consciously map your path. If you don't have it set to say *no* to resistance and complaints, then by default you may inevitably say *yes* to procrastination. If you've been saying *yes* to procrastination, it's important to get to the cost. Is procrastinating getting on your mat to practice yoga or meditation costing you the vitality, vibrancy, and health you want? Remember, to be a *yes* is to act.

Saying *yes* to the practice of saying *no* to the habits and thoughts that no longer serve you becomes a great source of strength and confidence.

In any pose, I'm always dealing with what is actually happening in my physical body. I can accept and empower what is so about my body or I can oppose and resist what's happening. Being *for* your body exactly as it is, and as it is not, is acceptance. The energy of *yes* is acceptance. Saying *yes* to accepting how things are and how they are not is a choice you make moment-to-moment, breath by breath. You can choose to be a *yes* for exactly how the pose is and how it is not, or you can oppose and resist. *Yes* holds the space for acceptance, and acceptance is the place from which you empower your body to generate some new result in the pose.

Being a *no* for what is happening in your body is opposition. Opposition produces tension in your body and manifests as rigidity in the pose, both physical and emotional. Ordinarily, if we experience strong sensations or physical limitations, we oppose what's happening in our body. To be against something is to be in reaction to it. In our body we experience that as stress, discomfort, contraction, and shortness of breath. We don't like that our bodies won't or can't do as we want, and emotionally, that leaves us with complaints, frustration, and resentment.

I've met many people who have faced serious health challenges and crises. Most went through an initial period of being angry, resentful, or even in downright denial about their illness—all perfectly understandable reactions. But the ones who I am always most amazed by are the ones who get to the idea that resisting what is so is actually causing them greater emotional suffering than the illness itself. Accepting what was going on allowed them to flow with the new demands of their bodies in a much more empowered way.

Acceptance of what is and is not happening—in a pose as in life—creates a mood of peace. As you engage in the dance of *yes* and *no* in the pose, you will discover that the muscles and the mood of your body becomes flexible and malleable in the energetic vibration of *yes*, and the experience of rigidity and unneeded hardness will begin to dissolve like ice in the warm sun.

Every student has his or her *no* pose. Maybe even more than one. You know your *no* pose: it's the one that makes you inwardly groan when the teacher calls it out, and likely leads you to automatically think, *Ugh . . . I don't want to . . . I can't do this one.*

But you actually don't know for sure that you can't do that pose. What you've come up against isn't necessarily a physical limitation. Resistance can be very deceiving behind the many masks it wears. Maybe you haven't been able to do that pose in the past, but what about today? The yogis say you can never step into the same river twice, because the current is always shifting and changing. You've never stepped into this exact river before today. Not with this body, not with today's particular energy, with the specific number of bites of breakfast in your belly, with the earth tipped on its exact axis. Perhaps up until now you haven't had a breakthrough in this pose, but that was then. What's possible *today*?

Every pose is a new opportunity, each and every time. All the work you've done up until now has been to lead you to this precise moment, to face precisely what you're facing. Yoga is a dance of dealing with what is, and allowing yourself to fully experience whatever you're experiencing right here, in the moment. In life, we so often resist what we don't like or don't want to do. Here, on your mat, is a safe opportunity to see what's on the other side of that. Physical asana is a measure of some higher possibility.

Put your attention on what you want to have happen and be for it, and watch the magic unfold.

What are you a *yes* for today?

You want to balance a practice that works with a practice that counts. The challenge is to recognize that just because you've gotten your practice to a place that works for you emotionally and physically doesn't necessarily mean that it matters. A practice that matters is tied to something deeper: the powerful, spiritual, alive energy of *yes*.

The only two forces at work in a pose are aliveness and patterns that block our aliveness. As patterns are dissolved and experienced out, our body becomes clearer and the flow from pose to pose begins to make more sense. It's funny, but when the more alive you emerges from behind the smokescreen of all those patterns of resistance (created by the energy of *no*) and begins to participate in the practice with resolution and directed focus of being a *yes*, the practice really does take on a purpose. It all somehow makes sense in a fantastic way.

There is no use searching externally for purpose, or trying to "pull it in." It is already available right here in the pose. Just focus on clearing out and letting go of what is between you and aliveness: your energy of *no*. Aliveness and purpose are practically the same thing and they are both created by *yes*. The purpose is greater aliveness, so every time we create greater aliveness, the purpose of the practice is being served.

The answer to how we create greater aliveness in our bodies and in our lives is always *yes*.

what you say is so

We are what we think. All that we are arises with our thoughts. With our thoughts, we make the world.

BUDDHA

One of my teachers, B. K. S. Iyengar, would say, "The asana begins the moment you want to come out of it." I couldn't agree more, because that's when the creative work happens.

Let's say you're in a pose and you get a strong body sensation. Your leg starts to quiver from the effort of Half Moon, or your hips are sounding alarm bells in Pigeon Pose. What do you do? Do you bolt? Or do you stay, adapt, breathe, flow, and grow?

Whether we stay or take ourselves out is determined by what we tell ourselves. We all have a default voice in our head that urges us to give up when the pose doesn't look like we think it should, when we don't get what we want or what we worked for, when it gets hard, when we fail. I've heard so many variations of what people tell themselves on the mat when things get challenging:

I can't.
I shouldn't.
I don't want to.
This is too much.
This pose is crazy/wrong/stupid; I don't need to do this.
I've done enough, no need to push it.
I'm the exception; this won't work for me.
I'm no good at this.

What does that voice whisper to you in the moment of giving up? The specific inner chatter that urges you to quit your flow is the signal that you've fallen into the default zone. You want to start paying attention to when you've entered your default zone, because recognizing it is where the possibility for transformation lies. A pose is the perfect opportunity to confront what you do when things get hard. When you're in a pose, you're in the action of life; your default will show up right away as soon as you're squeezed.

You'll notice that what comes up in the moment of giving up is a bunch of words. Just words. *You* give words their power. You act and don't act based on all the conversations in your head. You empower those conversations and then act accordingly. But consider that thoughts actually don't have to be directly connected to action. You have thoughts, but you are not your thoughts—and they definitely don't have to run the show. You can take conscious action in the face of any thought or inner conversation if you are alert and aware that it's there. You have all the power. *You* get to decide what you do in the moment of wanting to give up.

What would your practice (and your life, for that matter) look like if you did not empower the noise in your head? What if you relate to that conversation as just words and let it go, and stayed in the pose and in the flow?

The author don Miguel Ruiz said, "Your word is the power that you have to create. . . . It is through the word that you manifest everything. . . . The word is a force; it is the power you have . . . to create the events in your life."

Waking up to the habitual, disempowering things I would say to myself while in a pose was pivotal in my practice. It was a breakthrough for me to realize the impact of linguistics on my practice. Nothing really changed much for me in my practice until discovering that all transformation included a shift in my inner languaging. In fact, that was the key that determined whether I experienced a breakdown or a breakthrough on the mat.

Imagine you are on your mat, listening to the teacher give instructions to create a pose. You come into the pose and then hit a wall of some sort—difficulty, sensation, whatever it is that stops you—and you say to yourself, *I can't do this.* Chances are your inner dialogue doesn't stop there. Perhaps it continues on to something like, *I'm so weak . . . what's wrong with me?* That voice is not creative; it's reactive. It is the automatic default voice, commanding things to be or not be and influencing your every move, allowing or limiting what's possible in the pose.

When I first started to objectively observe that little voice in my head that says, *Enough of this,* or *I'm done,* I began to see its power over me. Over time, I became a skillful observer of myself, which freed me to choose pathways that were previously hidden from my view. I could choose new actions that were not unconsciously dictated by my default voice.

If you want to reach someplace new, you have to do something different than you've always done. Same actions will only yield the same results. Authentic new actions occur only when the observer within shifts, bringing new possibilities into view. When I reached the point of being able to shift my inner view and, from this new stance, really look and listen to what I was saying to myself in the pose, it was an opening to invite new actions toward new results. I didn't *have* to do what the default voice was dictating. I'd already tried that, and it got me only to where I was.

If new action is required for new results, then we need to make some new moves—what I call *language moves*. If I have a desire to positively alter my practice and create an alternative future, it is only going to happen through an embodied shift in my language. If I want a new experience in the practice, the inner work is to alter what I say—or, more precisely, to say things that I have not historically said to myself before and explore what happens.

What language moves can you take? What can you shift in what you are telling yourself to create a breakthrough? This is the art and mastery of yoga practice: look, listen, and work new tools to empower your desired results.

Once, while walking with the author Louise Hay, I was telling her a story and used the cliché "We could kill two birds with one stone." In her inimitable wisdom, Louise responded, "How about we go with 'Empower two birds at the same time'?"

What she was speaking to is the power of choice. We create our reality through what we say, both aloud and to ourselves. You have a very different experience just by what you tell yourself, because it sets the energy for what you're living into.

There's a story about two baseball umpires talking about a more seasoned umpire. One of the umpires says to the other, "Old Bill is a master. There are balls and there are strikes, and he calls them like they are." The other umpire responds, "Yes, Bill is a master umpire . . . there's balls and there are strikes, and he calls them like he sees them." In that moment, Bill walks up to them and says, "You are both wrong. There are balls and there are strikes, but they ain't nothing until I call them." The umpire speaks something into being, creating it to be what it is.

Just like the umpire, we have the authority to make declarations that direct how our world takes shape. Over the course of your life, you've made pivotal life decisions, both big and small. You've said *yes* to many things: perhaps a job, a relationship, becoming a parent. You've said *yes* to rolling out your yoga mat and practicing. Consider what it would look like if you had said *no* in any of those times when you said *yes*. How phenomenally different would your life be today? Can you see how your speaking *yes* or *no* determined the direction of your actions, creating possibilities and results? Can you see how saying *yes* or *no*, moment to moment on the mat, has impacted the results you have in your body and mind right now? Saying *yes* or *no* is a powerful act of closing one range of possibilities and opening an alternate range of others. Just through those two simple words, you enter some situations and move away from others.

We are always and in all ways constructing results out of what we say. At some level we already know this. It is the obvious, but it is so obvious that we often miss its power to profoundly transform a moment, a pose, or our lives.

Human beings assess everything. We assess ourselves and other people constantly. We assess our practice, our bodies, our emotions, our poses. This isn't good or bad, per se, but it does have an impact.

When our assessments live in our minds as "truth," we get stuck with them and whatever energetic vibration they create in our bodies. Since we are always already assessing, it makes sense to develop skillfulness in how we do so. Let's begin choosing to assess in ways that ground us and empower our practice, giving us access to the results we want.

The future impact of assessments we make now is often unseen. For example, let's say an aspiring yoga teacher named Jenny, who practices at her local yoga studio, joined my 40 Days to Personal Revolution program with a group of other yogis. And let's say Jenny ended up missing three yoga classes in a row for the first week. Let's say that actually happened—it is a *fact,* and her missing those classes could be proven *true* or *false.* On its own, that fact has no particular emotional flavor. It just is. Jenny missed three classes.

But, if we say, "Jenny missed three classes," and add that Jenny is unreliable and uncommitted, then this adds a subjective personal assessment about Jenny, which moves it toward a prediction of Jenny's future behavior and could alter other people's view of Jenny as a yogi and person. If I assess Jenny as unreliable and not committed, and in the future she wants to be on the senior teaching team at her studio, guess who the studio owner doesn't select? Jenny! Why? Because the assessment of her in the past as unreliable influenced others' view of her potential actions in the future. Our public persona gets created like this inside of community with others, but let's look at how we also do this to ourselves.

Typically when teaching a workshop I will have a full classroom of people, laid out mat-to-mat. That's a factual, verifiable description of the distance between mats and the number of bodies on those mats. If it is a large room, one might add the assessment that the room was spacious. Yet someone else could assess that the room was cramped. In both cases we could say that these are our subjective assessments, opinions, and judgments that form our beliefs about the room.

What if I said, "Alright, let's get to the truth here. What's the bottom line: Is the room spacious or is it cramped?" Some people might immediately agree with the assessment: "The room is cramped with people packed in like sardines!" Others may just as quickly say, "Well, anybody can see that the room is spacious with a lot of people intimately connected."

In reality, the room doesn't have a property in and of itself of spaciousness or cramped-ness. The room just *is*. In the realm of what I call *physicalness,* there is tangible measure. The room has a certain number of square feet within its walls, and we can count the number of bodies in the room. We can observe those measures and we can repeat those measures to others and they will hold them as true. "Spacious" or "cramped," on the other hand, are not measurable properties of the room. Whether it is spacious or cramped has everything to do with who's doing the looking and assessing.

So, while the observable measures in physicalness belong to the thing being observed (the room or the pose), we can say that opinions and judgments belong to the observer. This is a crucial difference. Distinguishing the observer from the thing being observed has huge impact on our relationship to the practice . . . and how we build and develop it, one pose at a time. When you begin to observe yourself as the observer of the pose, you can hear the beliefs and judgments you voice to yourself. These are the very same ones that get in the way of being in a creative relationship with your practice: how you work in the pose, how you problem solve, how you gauge your progress in a pose, how you interact with the pose on a multitude of levels.

You could say, for instance, "The pose is really hard," or you could say, "The pose is fancy." Well, which is it? Is the pose hard or is it fancy? Consider that the answer is purely within the eyes of the beholder. In physicalness, the pose doesn't have a property; in and of itself it isn't hard or fancy. The pose just *is*. Perhaps for me, I see the pose as hard, while another student may say it's fancy. Again, these are assessments that belong to the observer of the thing being observed, in this case the pose.

How many of us know people who act as if their assessments, personal opinions, and judgments are truth and fact? This is a common phenomenon. It is no surprise that people who view life as if their subjective assessments are The Truth have difficulty forming an empowering relationship with the practice and with life. There's no room for new possibility or perception if you are locked within your perception, holding it as the cold, objective, unmovable truth.

We experience new power and freedom when we begin interacting with what is so in the pose instead of with our assessments, judgments, and opinions. I call this the practice of *bare-bones physicalness*. When dealing only with the physical properties of the pose, we are in objectivity. Anyone else can verify the trueness or falseness, for instance, that my front knee is (or is not) stacked over my ankle in Warrior One pose, that my back foot is (or is not) flat on the floor, and so on. The facts about where my body parts are placed or the specific actions I'm taking in the pose are independent of my moods, emotions, and opinions. In bare-bones physicalness, I am in a dance with the physical reality of my body and not with my description and assessment of it.

Assessments reveal more about the observer than they do about the thing being observed. This is what I believe Mr. Iyengar was leading us to when he said the pose begins in the moment that you want to come out of it. Right here and now in the pose is an opportunity to learn something about yourself (the observer), and a chance to use language as a tool to transform your experience and yourself. The good news is that there is always space for another assessment if you allow for it.

It's good to know that how I assess the pose is greatly influenced by my personal standards, expectations, moods, and emotions. I could say that taking the pose is similar to waking up one morning and noticing there are no clouds in the sky, and it's 75 degrees out and no matter what mood or emotional state I am in . . . that is *so*. What I make of those facts is what determines how I perceive those conditions. Regardless of the weather, it's likely you won't hear me say, "It's a great day," unless I'm in a good mood!

A pose is not equal to an explanation, subjective assessment, mood, or judgment. This insight is crucial for redesigning our practice. It has nothing to do with whether or not my story (i.e., my assessment) about the pose is right or wrong. The shift happens when we take the opportunity to observe and ask, "Is my personal story I tell about this pose making me more or less powerful? Is this story I have about the pose working for me and allowing me to produce the results I say I want?" Because if it's not, I can learn, with time and practice, to create new stories that open up a new world and a new domain of possibilities on my mat and into my life.

the breath
of victory

What we call "I" is just a swinging door,
which moves when we inhale and when we exhale.

SHUNRYU SUZUKI

Your breath is the key to unlocking your body's potential. Maintaining steady, rhythmic breathing is the *single most important element* of yoga practice. The practice here is to begin to see your breathing in relation to the actions you're taking. It requires something extraordinary for any of us to really get to a true and connected relatedness to our breath, and the impact of it on our bodies, energy, and movement. As you become skillful at matching your breath to your movement, the two will no longer feel separate, but rather one thread that carries you through the fabric of your practice.

When used consciously, your breath becomes pure, raw energy that sweeps through you like a cleansing wind. With every inhalation, you bring new life into your body, with every exhalation, you clean house. As you breathe your way through your practice, you send signals to your brain that you are calm and safe. Matching and mirroring your movements with your breath, you peel away layers of physical and mental resistance. Your breath is what sustains you when you come to your edge in a pose, and allows you to move into new mental, emotional, and physical frontiers.

In Baptiste Yoga, the breath we use for asana practice is called *ujjayi*. Ujjayi breathing is the thread of breath force that elegantly weaves through the tapestry of our vinyasa practice. It is the access point to the source of serene passion required to intuitively lead yourself through your practice, and through your everyday life. Ujjayi serves as a source of equanimity and ease when the path gets tough. It is a doorway to vitality and creative energy.

The Sanskrit word *ujjayi* translates to "victory." In yogic principle, victory comes by being committed to something bigger than oneself. The question becomes: How do you create your practice to be about something bigger than yourself? The answer to that question is found in being aware of and tuned into the transformative power of your breath.

Breath and the absence of thoughts are correlated. By correlated, I mean a specific kind of connection in which breath, thoughts, and emotions are in a dance with one another. As you become conscious of your breath, you begin to notice it reflects your thought patterns, energy, and emotional moods like a mirror.

In my experience, most of us need a breakthrough in being conscious of our breathing, and our understanding of the impact it has on our practice. Most—if not all—of us are very poor observers of our breathing. Has this been your experience, perhaps? Most of us do what we do on our mats, and we produce positive results for the most part without really noticing our breathing. So the first step—the most important step— is to simply notice your breath. Try that right now; simply pause for a moment and notice your breath.

Observing breath is a tool to cultivate self-awareness. With every mood and emotion, your breathing has a different rhythm. When you are angry or frustrated, watch your breath; you will notice it has a certain quality. When you feel fear, observe how your breath responds. When you feel love, watch how the breath flows. When you are sad, notice the tempo and rhythm of your inhalations and exhalations. When you are calm, feeling happy, or just hanging out in Savasana, clue into your breath and see how it feels and sounds.

Have you noticed that when your body is healthy you breathe differently than when your body is sick? When you are ill, the breathing is off-center, or may alert you that something is wrong in the ecosystem within. In contrast, when you're in perfect health, you typically forget about your breathing because it flows without friction.

We are typically unaware of our breath, but the receiving pose is the perfect opportunity to get conscious of it. You get to know your breath patterns and their different qualities, and observe that whenever your state of mind changes, the breathing changes. The reverse is also true: change your breathing, and the state of mind and emotional energy changes. Breath awareness is a tool that has transformative powers; you can literally change your mind and your mood just through breath.

Pranayama is the practice of putting your attention on the breath and intentionally being at play with it. A big breakthrough awaits those who are at conscious play with their breath. When you bring your awareness to your breath while in the receiving pose, you are training the mind to hone its focus. Training yourself to keep your attention on your breath brings a meditative power to the pose and integrates the body, mind, and being. This cultivated mindfulness on the mat will then empower an overall ability to focus during everyday tasks.

In an article published in 2012 in the journal *Frontiers in Human Neuroscience*, researchers evaluated people who had no previous exposure to meditation. Some of the group were given 3 hours of mindfulness meditation training and were asked to meditate for 10 minutes each day for 16 weeks, and some of the group did not meditate at all. Both groups were then given tasks that involved attention to detail, and the meditators showed more control over executive functions. This study points to the possibility that even small amounts of meditation training can significantly change neural patterns in the brain.

The work for the newer yogi is to relate to the breath as something very interesting. Get really interested in its rhythm and effect, and you begin to create a new depth of relationship with your breath. Learn to just be with your breath in the pose. Observe it, and be at play with controlling the flow of breath into and out of your body. Observe the impact of your breathing on your physical structure, on the energetic vibration in your body. Do that and you will experience a sense of expansion. The simple act of observing your breathing will alter its flow, and as it alters, so will your ground of being.

•

The word *pranayama* is often translated to mean "breath control," but personally, I never liked that definition. I've discovered that pranayama is less about breath control and more about the expansion of energy and the flow of vitality that comes through conscious breathing. *Prana* means vital energy found in breath, and *ayam* means infinite expansion.

If, on the mat, the aim was to control the breath, that would put you and I in the role of "controller of life force," which diminishes what's possible in the vast landscape of pranayama. Pranayama offers a great expansion of your life force. Its gifts come when you become one with the flow of breath and experience it as part of the organic pulsation of your body, your emotions, and your energy. That might sound a bit like new-age fluff, but try it for yourself in the pose and see what happens. Allow your breathing to be a holistic, natural experience, in sync with the ebb and flow of your body's pulse and sensations and your energetic movement, and you'll see what I mean. This is how we break from "doing breathing" to being moved and used by the breath into an experience of total aliveness.

The goal of ujjayi breathing—the deep, rhythmic inhalation and exhalation used in yoga practice—is to do so in concert with the whole. This brings us to full presence and, very often, into harmony with those around us. This is true in a pose, or in life. I remember a time when I had first fallen in love with the woman I was going to marry. We were quietly sitting side by side on the beach in Del Mar, California, holding hands. We were in the experience of being really in love, and suddenly I became aware that we were breathing in unison. Without words, we were in a deep physical and emotional rapport, not breathing separately but as one. We weren't trying to inhale and exhale simultaneously; it just happened naturally.

Try this the next time you're sitting with a friend or loved one. Pay attention and you'll notice: if you're connected, you will likely be breathing together. If you are not connected, or there is agitation, you will likely be breathing separately. If you're sitting out in nature, meditating or just being quiet and enjoying being "out there" (i.e., outside your head) and at ease, you will notice your breathing is in sync with the sounds of nature around you. On the other hand, if you're in nature and lost in your mental commentary, there will be a disconnect from the pulse of nature, and your breathing will reflect that.

In a pose, if you are in true north alignment with your drishti—a soft, steady gaze—and your breathing is deep and free, you will become aware that your physical experience in the pose is flowing to the same rhythm you are breathing. You will notice that when breathing is happening as a holistic phenomenon, there is an absence of resisting and struggling. You have the experience of being surrendered, powerfully at ease and steady in the zone—so much so that there is no need to "do breathing," because you are already moving, breathing, and being from the center of the pose. You are in the experience of being whole, complete, and perfect, with nothing lacking or required.

Alternatively, let's say you are resisting, fighting, or struggling in the pose. Or you're bored, counting time until the pose ends. It would be a given, then, that you are breathing separately from the pose. True, you are breathing, but not in rhythm with your body, emotions, and experience. When you're dialed in and connected in the receiving pose, you will be breathing from and with your body; this can never happen when you are lost in the narratives and default conversations in your head.

This distinction of *in my head* vs. *in my experience* way of breathing is something I've discovered for myself from my as-lived experience on the mat. When you experience this for yourself, you will find that this energetic experience can be transferred and shared with others. In this way, the breath can transform not only us but our relationship to others.

When I was a kid, I traveled through India with my parents visiting many yoga and meditation masters. Each time, my father would say to me beforehand, "When you meet the master, always watch his breathing. If you feel a connection and relatedness to him or her, watch your own breathing, too." When meeting certain yoga masters, I would suddenly experience my breathing with full awareness, and my emotional mood would calibrate in tune with that master's breathing. I'd be left feeling deeply grounded in my body and connected to the core of my being.

Beyond being connected or disconnected to my own breath, or with another's, I've also had similar experiences on a group level. When teaching in a room full of yogis, I've felt what it's like to have my breath connected to each and every person in the room, all of us unified in a frictionless flow of breath. It flows from "me" to "we." As a teacher, if I am stuck in the confines of my head, not present and not leading from my body and being, I'll notice the breathing in the room is compartmentalized to each person and out of sync. If, however, I am outside my head and fully with them, authentically listening to the room, I will organically breathe with them, and them with me.

To me, pranayama means "to breathe holistically through your body, as a source of all movement and connection to others." This is the translation we use in Baptiste Yoga, in contrast to the common "control of breath." I believe that when we try to control the breath, we restrain it, and thus cut off the reservoir of vitality available to us. In the space of free-breath flow, your life energy expands you, on the mat and off.

●

The yogis say that in the gap between exhalation and inhalation—the place of "no breath"—you will find the secret of life. At face value, that assertion might seem absurd. Why look to a place of no breath to find the secret of life? No breath equals death, right? But it's a paradox. If you want to know life, you will be able to find it in the place of breathlessness. In that gap, there is no-thing; it is said that there you will find the energetic, creative source of life.

You can begin to do this by distinguishing the pause between the exhalation and the inhalation. That gap between breaths is your access point to the extraordinary and miraculous in your practice. In the receiving pose, after you inhale, take a conscious pause. Maybe play with holding the pause a little longer than usual and allowing yourself to feel the still space and vital energy. When you exhale, hold the pause in breathlessness a little longer than usual so you can experience the gap a little more deeply. Play with creating more time and spaciousness in your pattern of breaths in the pose.

One practice to alter your view and your emotional state is to play with stopping your breath for a brief moment. Anytime you are in a pose or even just taking a walk and realize you've drifted off into your thoughts, just stop the unconscious flow of breath and you'll notice in that pause you get jolted awake. The thoughts will stop immediately. This is a good practice because it demonstrates how breath and thoughts are correlated. When you rest in the pause of breath, thoughts disappear; you get present, and new possibility enters. Thoughts and breath are part of the physical world. No thoughts and no breath are part of the world of being, from which creation is generated.

There is great learning on the mat that comes from playing with the length of each breath in the gaps between breaths, but there is even greater power that comes from simply watching the whole process of breath as it comes in and out of your body. Watch: don't miss a single point as the breath comes in. Stay with it and you'll notice there is an automatic gap after the breath has entered. Be with that gap. Don't do anything; simply be a witness. As the breath begins to leave your body, continue watching. When it is completely out of your body and the breath stops, watch. Allow the breath to continue coming in, going out, coming in, going out, as you simply watch.

In those brief gaps, you'll immediately notice the thoughts disappear. When I say they disappear, I mean that your identification with them is broken, and in that opening, you can now point to them as being separate from you. You have them rather than them having you. You will consistently start to experience breath running parallel to thoughts coming and going in the mind. They are twin forces, as connected and opposing as two sides of the same coin. The process of watching the breath in the pose is where meditation and physical movement intermingle and meet up in real time in your poses.

The beauty of working with the breath is that it creates remarkable openings for people who are more body-oriented, as well as those who are more mind-oriented. Breathing practice is where the body and mind get aligned in the experience of being whole and complete. In my personal experience, it is not too much of a stretch to say that pranayama is the beginning and the end of yoga practice.

steady your gaze

*The sun's rays do not
burn until brought to a focus.*

ALEXANDER GRAHAM BELL

The Sanskrit word *drishti* means "gaze." Far more than just the act of beholding with your eyes, a steady drishti is one of the most powerful tools you can create as a yogi. Yoga practice is a meditation in action that is grounded through drishti.

Drishti occurs first in the observable, physical realm. Our physical eyes set on a specific physical point in the environment around us. From the beginning to the completion of each pose, relax your eyes and set them on a fixed point. Your eyes should be soft and tender. Hold your gaze steady throughout the pose, and, as you then move through the pose and then your vinyasa, reset your gaze consciously from point to point. A simple act, yet it yields powerful and profound results.

On a very practical level, a focused drishti is essential for stability in postures. A natural balance arises out of a calm mind, and it begins with the eyes. If your gaze is steady and focused, your mind will be, too, and you can effectively maintain your equanimity. This concentration of focus sends soothing messages to the nervous system and brings the mind from distraction to direction. Wandering eyes equal a wandering mind; focused eyes equal a focused mind. With a focused mind, you can accomplish extraordinary things. The eyes are the lens of the mind, and with drishti, you are focusing your consciousness in a practice of *pratyahara* (turning the senses inward) and *dharana* (focus and concentration on a task).

Pratyahara is the fifth limb of yoga, and has to do with bringing our senses into focus. Typically, in our normal life, our senses are all over the place. Rather than the mind commanding the senses—"look here!," "smell this!," "hear that!"—pratyahara funnels them toward one singular purpose. Let's say someone asked me a question, and I became involved in answering, growing more and more absorbed in my interaction with that person. That would create the state of pratyhara. Even though my eyes and ears are open, and my sense of smell and touch are fully functional, they fade into the background because I'm so involved in what I am hearing and saying. In pratyhara, the senses do not function in the usual sense due to the mind's involvement in something else.

Through drishti, we are training our senses to be used for one aim. For example, imagine you are sitting in meditation and you create a clear drishti by looking through the middle of your forehead with your eyes closed. You hold your attention on your hands and become completely absorbed in the ebb and flow of breath moving through your body, the pulsation of your heart, and alert to the sounds of your environment. In this perfect presence of peace and oneness, you would lose the sense that you are in a seated position.

When you come back to ordinary awareness, you may notice your legs fell asleep. It happens sometimes during meditation, but we may be less aware of that because our consciousness is directed toward the bigger purpose. The mind and the senses are working collectively, merged into the one experience of being present and awake to the moment at hand. In this way, pratyahara happens spontaneously. The practice of drishti, however, allows us to create the experience of pratyahara.

The sixth limb of yoga is *dharana*. Dharana is the state of mind where the mind (distinct from the senses) orients itself toward one point and nowhere else. It could be anything—a word, a sound, an object—but only one thing. Dharana is a stepping stone toward meditation. Dharana is not something you can do or create; it emerges spontaneously from drishti. When you've got your drishti, distractions fall away; internal chatter quiets; time stops (or at least your awareness of it). If you find yourself wobbling, falling, or asking, *"When is this pose going to be over already?,"* it's a sign you've lost your drishti.

Drishti also generates *tapas*, which is a cleansing, purifying heat. The internal energy of tapas embodies the physical properties of heat: it rises, expands, softens, melts, and evaporates. The powerful tapas generated by drishti can burn away hesitancy, fear, and resistance, clearing your internal landscape of limiting views and giving you access to full self-expression. If you try to reshape cold glass, it will shatter. Heat it and you can form it, bend it, and shape it in any way you want. The energetic fire of tapas creates a similar result in your body and on your resistance. Fire it up and it becomes pliable.

A focused gaze, grounded in a singular point, frees you from judgments and the flurry of mental assessments. It transports you to the clear space of the receiving pose, where all fundamental transformation happens. Drishti gives us access to the eighth limb of yoga, known as *samadhi*, which translates to "neutral vision." *Sama* means "even" or "neutral," and *dhi* means "vision" or "seeing." Neutral vision means to see without judging. No appreciating nor condemning; simply looking. Samadhi is to see through a clear lens, rather than viewing your experience through the rearview mirror of past perceptions. Cultivating samadhi on your mat will help you bring that quality of mind into your everyday life.

Still another level of drishti's powerful effect is this: where you put your attention is where energy will flow. If you dwell on your challenges in life as though they really are part of you, that's what you'll generate in your life. If you focus on where you are going and what you are committed to in your life, that's what you'll create right now. Through physical asana, you practice maintaining your steady focus, from physical point to physical point, and building body alignment and awareness that empowers you well beyond the time you spend on your mat. Your work through drishti can deeply and dramatically change your entire experience of life.

Drishti is sometimes referred to as our third eye: the uncolored, unfiltered perception attained through the lens of our consciousness. In Baptiste Yoga, we say that the art and mastery of our practice comes from our ability to authentically *look* and *listen*. We learn to steady the gaze in each pose to train the mind and to engage more powerfully in the practice.

In order for you to be able to authentically look within the receiving pose, you will need to first recognize and acknowledge the automatic, past-derived default perceptions that get in the way of genuinely creating your practice, moment by moment. You'll need to shelve what you know about the pose, what you believe to be true about it, what your past experience tells you about it; you want to clear all that away. You want to get your drishti to the place where there is nothing between you and the pose at hand. You don't have to throw away all your valuable knowledge and learned experience; you just need to get it out of the way so that there is no content between you and what you are dealing with on the mat, pose to pose. As you become more skillful at steadying your gaze, you'll gain the capacity to hold on to what you already know and allow it to shine light on this moment without it eclipsing the blank canvas of new creation.

The writer Anaïs Nin said, "We don't see things as they are. We see them as we are." What settles us into one (limiting) perspective is seeing things only through our positions, opinions, rationalizations, and history—that is, through the filters of what we think we know. That becomes the place from which we "look" in the pose. And because for us what we see from that perspective seems to be "the way it is," we get stuck in that way of seeing. Having nothing between you and the pose means you are looking through a clear lens—an uncolored drishti—and relating to the bare-bones, as-lived, real-time physical and energetic experience. When there is nothing between you and whatever is coming up for you in the pose, you will have the experience of seeing what arises from a myriad of perspectives.

To be masterful in the practice, you have to be willing to drop what you know as "the truth" and what your past experience tells you, and acknowledge that that is simply one way of looking at things. The mastery comes from expanding your drishti from one default view to a panoramic 360-degree view.

Setting the point of your gaze and being with your actual experience in the pose allows you to free yourself from the grip of your default perspective so that you are able to see what is revealed about the pose,

your body, and your experience from varying perspectives. Automatically, a multitude of pathways and
possibilities open up when there's nothing between
your "looking" and what you are interacting with
on the mat.

Drishti is more than just staring at a spot on the
wall. It's an open-eye meditation of really seeing what
you're seeing and being with that focal point.

You connect to that point out there, and from that
point, you'll notice that your connection to all your
inner points expands. One point gives us access to all
points. When you really have your drishti, suddenly,
you "get" your feet; you get connection and access to
your breath; you get access to your core.

Set your eyes to one point in front of you; try that
now. You'll notice that when your gaze is clear and
empty of content, you suddenly get access to other
things. From that one focused point out there in your
physical environment, simultaneously notice another
point—say, your feet and their contact to the floor.
Then your legs and their contact to your pelvis, up
through your torso, out through your arms into your
hands, up your neck to the crown of your head. Now,

as you gaze to one point, keep that awareness and also notice the ebb and flow of breath into and out of your chest.

From that singular point, expand your awareness to whatever emotion is present for you here in your experience, and where that emotion is located in your body. Is it in your chest, your shoulders, your belly? You can keep adding points of awareness from your singular point. The main thing to learn here is that your one clear gaze, held steady to a point, opens up a whole world of other points. You get access to parts of yourself, your body, and your experience that you can connect to and begin to shape and shift . . . all from the one point we call "drishti."

If you want to change your mind, change your gaze.

If you stand at the bottom of the Grand Canyon, it looks much different than if you stand at the edge of the upper rim looking in, just like turning upside down and standing on your head makes the world appear vastly different than when you are standing on your two feet. Where you stand—both in physical space and within your body—impacts what you see. It impacts what is known as the observer: the you that sees with neutral vision.

Drishti allows for a physical grounding and allows us to inquire from the observer perspective. It allows us to ask, "Am I seeing this experience from a default lens, filtered through my past experience, or am I trying on new views?" Setting your physical gaze creates the space to shift your vision from default to neutral (and thus opening the possibility for the new) in any moment.

A student once shared with me her breakthrough in drishti. She said she had been struggling with her balance in Dancer's Pose for many months and was trying to figure out what to do to correct that, but nothing seemed to be working. After trying several adjustments and so on, none of which seemed to make any difference, she felt like there just weren't any new possibilities available to her to "fix" this pose.

At some point during a class I was teaching (this was before I knew her backstory), I noticed her struggling in Dancer's Pose. The ankle of her standing leg was wobbling and she fell out of the pose several times, visibly frustrated. I walked over to her mat and suggested that she focus on firmly pressing down through the center of her heel and the mound of her big toe and pull up and tighten through her centerline and core. I repeated several times, "Set your eyes on the horizon, press the floor, and lift up into your core."

Suddenly, her whole body and being got trued up to center, and the pose manifested into an easeful state of balance. She was totally lit up and, from that beautiful natural expression of Dancer's Pose, broke out in a huge smile! Clearly this was an aha moment for her. My fresh perspective provided her with a new alternative that had always been available to her; she just wasn't seeing it. She got a new drishti—a view from true north alignment—that allowed for a new possibility in her practice.

Later, after class, this woman said to me, "It was amazing how my gaze gave me access to the bottom of my foot pressing down into the floor, all the way up to my core. Up until now, I just wasn't getting what that meant, but now I see what you were saying!" Most of us have had some kind of similar experience with something that we had been struggling with in a pose or in life. At some point, a teacher or another person's insight comes along, and this new observer offers a different perspective that allows us to break through to a new way of seeing.

I've learned that how we do anything or how we handle ourselves in a pose or situation has a great deal to do with the kind of observer we are. We assume that our results have to do with the actions we take, and of course that's true and obvious, but what's less obvious is that our actions themselves are deeply tied to how we see things. The way we see things comes before any action we take.

One aspect of drishti is how we frame a situation, in the pose or out. Our default drishti might just see our limitations and what's not possible, and keep us caught up in the struggle, much like what had been happening with this student in Dancer's Pose. The way we frame a situation creates or limits what's possible. Our *yes* will always come from what's possible, as seen by the observer we are in that situation.

So all this is to say: when you feel stuck or frustrated, it's a sign that you are caught in a clouded vision of observer. There is always another perspective, always another possibility. Reframe you as the observer through drishti, and through shifting your vision, you'll change your mind, your actions, and your results.

We think we need to go inward to get someplace good, or sacred, or connected, but we have it 180 degrees backward. We must gaze outward to get connected inward. I know this may land for you as counterintuitive, but consider there is something extraordinary for you to discover "out here," rather than "in there" (i.e., inside your head). The path to the goodies available to us "out here" is through your drishti.

I know that in my work, if I want to be out in the world and do the things that I want to do, I actually have to get out of my head. All my thoughts, emotions, and sensations swirl together to make an internal stew, and then the meaningful connections, insights, and inspiration that are "out there" aren't available to me because I'm stuck in that internal muck. To get a new sense of myself and what is possible, I have to go beyond my internal walls. I've got to really see what's around me . . . smell the flowers . . . really connect and be with others to get a whole other sense of myself. And the path to that enlightened vision is through drishti.

drop, stream, river

Life is a series of natural and spontaneous changes.
Don't resist them—that only creates sorrow.
Let reality be reality. Let things flow naturally
forward in whatever way they like.

LAO TZU

Vinyasa means "flow." In vinyasa yoga, there is a seamless current running from pose to pose, breath to breath, start to finish. There is no pause of movement, only fluidity between one pose and the next. In this way, vinyasa highlights the yogic principles of *pratyahara* (turning the senses inward), *yama* (being led by greater direction of movement), *niyama* (focused concentration to apply the methodology with skillfulness), and *dhyana* (meditation, a surrender to the greater whole and to what calls you). As you experience surrendering to these principles, physical and mental resistance dissolves and you find yourself melting into the greater whole of flow.

The Buddha says you can be a drop of water, a stream, or the raging river; it doesn't matter which as long you're in the flow, because they are all moving toward the ocean. In vinyasa flow, you are inwardly pulled toward something greater than yourself—your inner ocean, so to speak.

We could say that yoga is the point where many aspects of a person merge together in one flow toward some new point. In our practice, that means to converge the movement of the mind, body, breath, and spirit in the pursuit of that inner ocean. When we integrate all the aspects of who we are and organize and orient ourselves from that integration, we have our true north alignment, and suddenly we experience ourselves in flow, taken by something greater than ourselves.

Another aspect to the meaning of yoga is to reach a point we have not reached before. Let's say there is something that is impossible for you to do today. Perhaps you're stuck in how to make a pose work for you, or at an impasse in your work or in your relating to another person. Then you do the work and find a pathway that enables you to break through, and what you've been aiming for suddenly becomes possible.

The intentions, actions, and energy you corral toward manifesting that possibility into reality are all examples of what it means to "do yoga."

In fact, any movement to create something new, like finding a way to touch your toes or correlate your breathing with your movement, or gaining a new insight about yourself through purposeful inquiry and dialogue, is yoga. In any situation in which you've taken yourself to a new place with passion and purpose, you are living as a yogi.

There is one more classic definition of yoga, which is to be one with something greater or bigger than ourselves, regardless of what name we use: God, a higher power, the universe, and so on. Any movement in our body, any words we speak, or thoughts we think that unites us with this experience of something higher than ourselves is an expression of yoga.

Why am I telling you all of this, you might be wondering? Because at the heart of all of these definitions and aspects of yoga is the vehicle through which you reach these states, and that is flow. Letting go and surrendering to flow gives you access to powerful new possibilities for expansion and mastery.

●

You already have flow. It's not something you need to attain or create; it's natural to you, already a part of who you are. Your work is to simply remove the obstacles that block it.

Once these obstacles are removed, we see we have always had what we sought: the ability to be in the experience of pure flow on the mat and in life. It was there all along, but was simply impeded. It is truly a transformation at the core of your being when you get clear that nothing has to be added for you to have flow. You were never lacking anything in your practice or in your life. In fact, you possess too many things that are not needed. You are so much and have so much, and yoga calls upon you to drop something and allow flow.

In essence, to have flow is to let go, lighten up, and surrender. Imagine if you set out to climb a mountain. The higher you climb, the more you will feel the weight of the gear you are carrying on your back. Your baggage will start to feel heavier and heavier as the terrain gets steeper and the air grows thinner. Eventually, you may reach a point where you need to leave some things behind to drop the extra weight to allow yourself to reach the highest peak.

When you drop the weight, you gain a lightness and bounce in your step. You begin to enjoy the climb rather than struggle against it. Suddenly, you feel free and the whole climb becomes about your body, your breath, and your mind working in harmony to make the climb. You are freed up to put all your energy toward supporting what you are up to, which is reaching the peak.

•

You know you have flow in your practice when there is the presence of direction, intentionality, precision, and total surrender—all at once.

Think of your mat like a raft on the river. Surrender and go where the current, the bigger flow takes you. In deep surrender, the mind and all the extra chatter disappears. When the default mind is not at work, we become aware—perhaps for the first time in our practice—of something that has always been there in being and spirit.

There are two opposing qualities to asana that work in concert: *sukha* and *sthira*. Sthira is effort, firmness, stability, and action. Sukha is receptive, spacious, relaxed, and surrendered. Sukha is the main quality of flow. The more you fight and resist, the more you muscle through a pose, the more you will create obstructions in the flow.

Surrender is what vinyasa is all about. And yet, in my experience of teaching over the last few decades, people resist going with the flow. Giving up control has little appeal in a culture of high achievers. They will ask for help becoming more confident in their poses, for help in having more stamina, or help feeling more empowered. Rarely will someone ask how to give anything up, or how to surrender. But consider that through surrender there is the possibility of discovering a whole new kind of power beyond any that you can muster up yourself.

The experience of flow can feel graceful and effortless when things are moving along just the way we'd like. We've all had the experience of being on our mat in practice and our bodies, breath, and energy are all working together in harmony to enable us to take the physical forms we want in the way we want to.

But we also know that yoga is a perfectly imperfect practice, and the very next day we may hit a plateau that can slow us down or even stall us indefinitely. You know you have flow in your practice when you reach such a plateau and don't automatically react with frustration or anger. You can trust that you are still in the stream (even if it's slowed to a trickle), and that things will pick up again toward your destination. Just being with the process as it is, is the act of being in flow. Some plateaus are brief, and others long. Either way, you stay, knowing it is part of the greater flow on the mat and in life. You know you have flow in your practice when you can respond to a break in speedier tempo or achievement with power and insight, leveraging the slowdowns as openings for greater mastery.

•

Flow emerges in your practice when your poses become an expression of yourself, rather than just a reproduction of what others have taught you or a duplication of mechanics. The poses become yours: *your* Tadasana, *your* Wheel Pose, *your* Savasana, whatever that may look like. Flow releases and inspires your inner artist and allows you to create something unique to you in the pose, and in the transition between the poses.

The most valuable thing you can do in the receiving pose to awaken that inner artistry is look and listen. Sometimes it's for possibility: Where can you go deeper? What's available to you in this moment? And sometimes, you'll need to look and listen for what's missing. What tools can you apply that will make the difference for you right now? Drishti? A modification? Breath? (Very often, it's breath. Forgetting your breath is the fastest way to block flow.)

There's nothing wrong with taking Child's Pose, of course, but you don't have to completely come out of a pose to make it work for you and remain in the flow. What can you adjust in your technique? What can you re-create? Can you drop a knee, use a block? It's tempting to fall into default and quit when a pose gets challenging—to just stop and take yourself out of the flow completely. That's fear running the show and telling you to give up. Instead of taking yourself out entirely, though, you always have the option to stay in the dance and work at just 20 percent if that's all you can do on this particular day. The question to ask is whether your level of work is determined by reality, fantasy, or fear. Of course, we are dealing with physiology, and each of us has a responsibility to take care of our bodies. But if 20 percent is all that is available to you, why not do that, fully and wholeheartedly? The practice here is to remain in the flow and honor your body's physicality and, at the same time, be starkly honest with yourself if you're being stopped through responsibility for caring for your body.

Years ago, a woman came to a Level One bootcamp I taught in Mexico. On the third night, as she was leaving the dining hall, she tripped and sprained her ankle. At first, she was really upset and angry about it. She'd come all this way to participate in seven days of rigorous practice and learning, and her plans were thwarted. We've all had our own version of this experience, haven't we? In any event, after we iced and bandaged her ankle, she declared she was going to stay and see out the week, even if she couldn't practice.

For the next four days, my staff made sure to make this woman comfortable as she lay on her mat during our practices, propping up her injured ankle with blankets. Lying down was literally all she could do, but wow was she in a powerful practice! She shared with us at the end of the week that she learned so much that week by *not* doing the poses, and instead getting connected to the bigger picture of the practice and its meaning. She explained that she entered a whole other dimension of yoga and learning about herself that went way beyond the physical form of the practice.

This woman was able to surrender to the "plateau" she found herself on, and in doing so, saw that the plateau was just physical. It didn't mean that she as a person was stopped or stumped in any way, and she felt a patience with the process that she had never experienced before. She went on to say that she had never felt comfortable in her own body; in fact, she'd always felt like a slave to it. For the first time that week, she felt totally at home in her own skin. She was amazed that this transformation didn't happen out of doing more, or trying harder, but rather through a total surrender to the flow of life and energy that was already available to her.

When you are moved by the bigger picture, you will naturally hold yourself accountable, because you will love making the highest call at each step and getting that much closer to the ocean. When you are committed to living and expressing from your truth—your commitment to your higher purpose—you'll know what's needed in each moment. Work within what is so, with power and responsibility. That's the balance we seek on our mats and in life, moment to moment.

Be a drop, a stream, or a raging river—it doesn't matter which form you take, as long as you remain in the flow.

be where you are

Face the facts of being what you are,
for that is what changes what you are.

SØREN KIERKEGAARD

We live in a world that teaches the importance of
ambition, efficiency, expediency, getting things done
to produce the quickest results. It does not teach or
encourage us to relax and just be where we are. In fact,
if we are not crazy active and doing a million different
things, we get labeled as lazy or unambitious. As a culture, we are uber-active, always trying to reach somewhere. The irony is that for the most part, nobody
knows exactly where they are trying to reach. We're
obsessed with trying to go better and faster to get there,
without really knowing exactly where "there" is.

Not surprisingly, we bring this paradigm to the
mat. Sometimes while teaching, I will walk around the

class and approach someone who looks like they are really struggling and trying hard. I'll quietly ask, "Just checking in, and curious about where are you trying to get to in the pose?" Typically the response will be something like, "I'm not sure where I'm going exactly but I'm doing my best." I get that. In a way, that's all of us. Our whole life we've been going somewhere, but just like in the pose, we don't know where we are going . . . not really, at least not in the big picture.

We keep looking to get anywhere other than right here where we are. Being where you are is a scary place for most. Can you be where you are and not freak out? Can you go to that scary place called *right here where you are* and not meddle, interfere, or need to fix anything? On the mat is the opportunity to be where we are totally, intimately, and wholeheartedly, and from that space allow the next move, the next possibility to arise.

Right now you might be thinking, *Well, of course I want to get somewhere. I don't want to just be stuck where I am. I want to do the work and get someplace new in my practice!* Yes, of course you and I and all of society are wired to work and to get results, and we know how to do that. Even in Baptiste Yoga we use the slogan "Don't wish for it, work for it." Yet in our workaholic society, we don't have any counterbalance. We don't have access to our ability to be just where we are, as we are. There is one word that sums up our ability to be where we are: *relax*. We haven't learned how to relax with what is.

I am not telling you not to do the work or to just hang out in Child's Pose. I am asking you to allow yourself the space to relax with yourself and be where you are wholeheartedly and see what arises from that. Consider that you can only really exceed yourself if you can first relax with yourself, right where you are— on the mat, in the pose, and in your life.

•

If we aren't satisfied with how our pose looks or feels, we tend to resist what is so. We become frustrated that we are not better, even resigned or cynical. When we move and breathe from a perspective of *This isn't it . . . I'm not where I want to be . . .* , we experience emotional resistance that can feel energetically stuck and impossible to break through. Yet the resistance itself is precisely what keeps us stuck there. We are resisting what and where we are, which yields more of the same.

The clear acknowledgment and acceptance of *what is* reveals ground zero for growth. We are not wired for and have not been trained to do that in the modern world, so acknowledging (and even appreciating) the raw truth of where you are is revolutionary. That revolution disrupts the complacency or overdrive in your practice and puts you on a track to a new creation.

Say, for instance, we take Warrior III Pose. There is that brief moment just after setting it up and stepping into it where our mind is clear and we experience "now here." This moment is the receiving pose. It is the extraordinary flash of full presence and expression for which we practice—and it is also the moment where most of us disempower ourselves by interacting with the mental noise in our heads. Our legs are quaking, and the sheer exertion of holding most of our body on a horizontal plane is simply uncomfortable, but the physical demands are not what get us. We begin to hear those familiar default thoughts of *This isn't it . . . I'm not doing it right . . . Screw this . . . I'm out of here. . . .* We begin interacting with our resistance in the pose instead of the bare-bones experience in our bodies.

It is at this juncture that we can consciously decide who we will be in the pose. We can choose to keep what we've mentally constructed about ourselves and our experience in Warrior III, along with our explanations and justifications about why we shouldn't go deeper or stay longer. We can even keep our complaints and our rightness about our complaints. Keeping all that is not necessarily bad or wrong. It's just one path, which over time is likely to become a habitual dead-end path called *How it is for me in Warrior III.*

Or, we can recognize our limiting mental constructs and be 100 percent for them, and clear about what they yield, expecting nothing less and nothing more. In other words, we can get real with ourselves. We can look, listen, and accept what is so in our experience in the pose—in our bodies, our emotional energy, and our thoughts. This immediately connects us more deeply to what is actually happening in our body and experience, and from there we can give ourselves tools to empower us in the pose right here, right now. That is the art of conscious creation.

In the moment of receiving the pose, if we act from *This should be different, or better than it is,* we are interfering with the natural energetic flow and impeding what's possible in the moment. If we are oriented around our narrative or justification of why we can't, won't, or don't want to, we are in a domain where there is no velocity, no freedom, no power to generate and organically create.

Trusting our as-lived experience in the pose, on the other hand, frees us to act even in the face of our resistance. From a place of kindness, we can acknowledge any resistance or thoughts of *This pose isn't enough as it is.* Allow for total acceptance of what is and what is not, and you will notice your energetic heaviness dissolve. From this new lightness, you can make a conscious connection to each point in your body and start to play in the pose, generating it as a joyful and creative self-expression, no matter what form it takes.

Whatever comes up in a pose, and whatever comes along, is merely something for you to be with and experience. It is so simple and straightforward: let your resistance be, and it will let you be. This approach expands your being and allows for the extraordinary to enter. The creative flow in the practice will expand because *you* expand. Resistance dissolves in the face of full acceptance, and you are transported into a whole new world.

We have a responsibility in our practice to be straight with ourselves. I don't mean necessarily just being responsible for the physical facts of your ability, but rather being intentional and skillful in your ability to respond to your experience of what is so.

If you know you can go further and dig deeper and just don't, then just take responsibility for that. Not with judgment, but simply acknowledgment. Making yourself wrong for it puts you on a whole other track. Just own it and be with it, as it is. Even if the story you tell yourself about why you can't or won't is valid and true, acknowledging it allows you the space to decide if you want to continue to rely on it, or choose another action.

When you really get to the idea that being exactly where you are is the key, that's when you step outside the box you've been in. Your pose may not change, but your whole experience of it will change. There is *so* much available to you in whatever form of the pose you're in, but you'll never know if you're struggling against it.

There's a difference between accepting where you are and making excuses for hanging back. But really, *you know*. You know when you're making up a story and resisting. Again, just be straight with yourself here, without judgment. Are you genuinely being where you are, or are you letting yourself off the hook and slipping into the energy of no? You've got to get real to get to the good stuff.

Tell the truth about where you are. Whatever it is, wherever you are in your practice, whatever your fear or limitations . . . just own them. That's the secret to creating a new way, a new path, a new pose, a new practice.

What does accepting "right now" look like in a pose? When you truly experience right here, right now in your body and are aligned to the rhythm of your breath, you see it is all perfect exactly the way it is. When I am being myself, nothing more and nothing less . . . when I am present and allowing what is happening within and around me to be exactly like it is . . . when I am being in the moment instead of being fixed on where I am going . . . when I am observing it all just as it is without having to figure it out and adding any assessments or comparisons, then I observe that all is perfect.

The ability to be where you are in your body begins with your ability to respect your body. That means accepting, loving, and deeply appreciating your body's complexity and magnificence, and being grateful for all it does for you. That also means being willing to listen to and follow your body's cues. Once you start authentically listening and communicating with the moods, sensations, and experiences of your body, your practice becomes very easeful. Working from being where you are, not from trying to get somewhere, you can work organically with the energy and capacity available to you. You won't need to fight with your body, or force it in any way; that just creates more tension and takes you out of flow. You don't have to force your body to do something, because it actually *wants* to work for you. But all of this requires that you be right there where you are and tune into what your body needs while in the pose.

When I am in a pose, I am in a communication with my body. If I make that communication conscious and intentional, then something extraordinary can happen. In the pose there is no need to try to dominate your body. Simply listen to it. Once you really tune into it, the imbalances, holding patterns, and pockets of locked up emotion and stuck energy will begin to disappear.

Unfortunately, many people don't really listen. In a demanding pose, the body may say, *Stop. Don't push any further.* But if the default mind says, *Don't stop. You need to push harder,* guess which voice gets heeded? On the mat and in life, we don't listen to the body; the default mind too often dictates and overrides it. Case in point: Have you ever been eating and your body signals, *That's enough; you don't need any more,* while your mind says, *Just a little more?* We've all been there at one time or another. We don't listen to the wisdom of the body and the consequence is that body gets imbalanced. Listening to your body happens in the moment as a conscious interaction.

You will be surprised that if you can relax with yourself and simply be where you are in the pose, it will give you a deeper insight into yourself. Being relaxed and present with where you are has transformative power and will alter the quality of the work you do on the mat. You will have an equanimity emanating from your center in every pose; your practice will be creative, not reactive. It will be more artistic, graceful, and skillful, and less stressful. You will notice you are less tired, less tense, less awkward than you used to be, because now you are more connected and centered at your core.

And if you can do that for 30, 60, 90 minutes on the mat, you will discover that even while doing hard work your body is at ease, your mind is relaxed, and your heart is open. Be where you are and melt into that experience and you will find that instead of having to recover from your asana practice, your body, energy, heart, and emotional intelligence recovers during the practice. All the frantic and unnecessary doing will drop away, and there will be new sharpness, precision, and flow. You will not be fidgety. You will simply do what needs to be done in the pose and in the moment: clearly, directly, exactly, and intentionally. That efficiency of energy that will transform you and transport you to beautiful places and expressions in your practice that are authentic and unique to you.

The technique of being relaxed where you are, as you are, is very simple.

Your body has profound wisdom if you simply listen, relax with it, and trust it. In every pose, trust that your body knows what it needs and that it will tell you, in contrast to you telling it. If it needs more integration from your extremities to your core, it will begin to activate the appropriate muscles to pull into your centerline. If it needs more oxygen, it will naturally begin to breathe from more depth and fullness and in rapport with your body movements. The less you interfere, the more you will be moved by the wisdom of your body. In this approach there is grace and beauty, and an inner sunlight radiating out through your posture.

As soon as you snap into not being okay where you are, you will stop trusting the natural body process and start trying to fix your pose and "get it right." Notice how when you resist being where you are on the mat you get caught up exerting a lot of unnecessary effort, and thus lose vitality. The ease vanishes.

As you allow yourself to be where you are, you will gain the sensitivity to see how far to push and when to let be. There are times to push upstream and there are times to let go and follow the river downstream. Being where you are allows for the wisdom of your body to emerge and for you to get intimately connected with it—to experience your body not as a "fixed thing," but rather as a dynamic, living, moving process.

If you want to get anywhere genuinely new, it will require that you be totally present where you are first. So if you do a pose you don't like or that causes you to be uncomfortable, do it from where you are and not where you wish you were. Do the pose with all of your heart and being until you become deeply connected to your experience of it, allowing the wisdom of your body to lead you. Be in awe of how it suddenly becomes a total experience of yoga for you. Relaxing with what is allows you to become wholly immersed and one with the pose. Yoga is an experience—a living, breathing, moving experience. If you can simply do the pose and do the practice without the "yogi" or practitioner dominating or calling the shots, that pose becomes yoga; it becomes meditative. Meditate but don't become a meditator, because the meditator starts manipulating the experience, focusing on the proper application of tools and techniques and thus losing the experience of being totally immersed and present. Lose yourself to find yourself in the pose.

If we are not connected to and in deep communication with our body, we are not in contact to the earth and the forces of nature that we are meant to be in tune with. Once you allow yourself to be where you are, you will get rooted in your body. From there, anything and everything becomes possible.

begin again

*Be not the slave of your own past ... plunge
into the sublime seas, dive deep, and swim far, so
you shall come back with new self-respect, with
new power, and with an advanced experience
that shall explain and overlook the old.*

RALPH WALDO EMERSON

Physicality is an observable, measurable thing. Your body can do whatever it can do; it can reach whatever thresholds it can right at this moment. The problem and loss of power comes in when we invent stories about those physical facts:

I can't do that because I'm not strong enough. I'll get hurt.
I'm too stiff and locked up.
This class is too hard for me.
I deserve to take it easy. I had a hard day.

All of these are typical default reactions, automatically generated by the mind when we go unconscious. Instead of fully being in the experience of the pose, we start talking to ourselves about it. To shift your practice—and your experience of your practice—you want to get powerful in snapping out of the trance. Wake up and recognize that you're in your head, and come back "out here." By "out here," I mean the present moment—the true, unfiltered reality of what's actually happening in your body on your mat right here, right now.

I had a student once who came to a weeklong teacher training with a headache. Not just any headache—it had been going on for the better part of a month by the time she arrived that first day. Second day of the training, same headache. On the third day, we talked about the distinction between "in here" (meaning inside your head) and "out here," and she made a conscious effort to really tune into my voice as I was teaching. Rather than focus on the fatigue in her front leg in Warrior Pose, or wrestle with her inner *When is this going to be over?* chatter, she affixed her gaze to a single physical point "out here" in the room, and focused on the ebb and flow of her breath and the sound of my voice, all of which connected her to her body movements, her hands, her feet, her core, her physical and energetic flow. At some point during the practice, she realized the headache had disappeared.

Nothing about my voice or what I was teaching dissolved her headache; I don't have magic powers. It was the shift in her awareness that did. A little while later, she noticed the headache came back. But she also noticed she'd drifted off again, wandering around inside her thoughts. Each time going forward when she felt the headache, it was a signal to begin again, refocus her attention back "out here," reset her drishti, bring in breath, root her feet to the floor, and locate herself within her measurable, observable, physical environment, and get present. In other words, to come back to her true north alignment.

The cycle of going unconscious and waking up is a practice of simply beginning again. We're always in process with this. The moment you wake up and realize you've drifted off into thoughts and storyland, you simply connect to your senses, open your eyes and your ears, feel your feet on the floor, plug in to the physical world "out here," and begin again. You come back to presence and start over.

Will you drift off again? Yes, of course. Every time you notice you've drifted off into your head, just go through the process of locating yourself in physical space ("I feel my feet on the floor right here . . . I see what I see and hear what I hear in the physical space around me") and begin again. You may need to start over moment after moment, and that's okay. There is no place else you are supposed to be—the place to be is here, where you are.

You are developing a new muscle; have faith that the gaps between needing to begin again will get bigger and longer. Maybe only by a millisecond at first, but they will. And in those gaps is a space of pure possibility. Just keep doing it. Repetition is the mother of mastery. That's why this is called a practice, not an arrival.

If you fall out of a pose—and we all fall sometimes—simply reestablish your true north alignment in your body, breath, and being and begin again. No story, no drama, no embarrassment, no fuss. Confucius said, "Our greatest glory is not in never falling, but in rising each time we fall." Begin again is the practice of gracefully rising and re-directing every time we fall away from our true aim.

If you realized you've spaced out during your practice and are just going through the motions, that's a good thing—you've woken up. Simply reset your drishti and begin again. Don't worry about what you've missed; keep your gaze fixed to what you're now creating in this present moment, and the next, and the next.

If you realize you've fallen out of integrity with yourself and your commitment to practice, well done. You've seen through the cloud of unconsciousness to clarity, and opened the portal of your awareness to step on your mat and begin again, with new intentionality.

In life, the instant you recognize you've gone astray, lost your way, or fallen out of alignment can be painful, but it can also be golden. Because in there lies the opportunity to redirect and begin anew.

•

At the deepest level of making a real difference in your practice of asana and meditation, you can practice the slogan "begin again" as a way to shift away from resistance and distraction and return to your true aim in the pose. We can say a lot of things about this practice or presence, but the crux of its purpose is you becoming empowered and able to dissolve what stands in your way, press the reset button, and begin anew—fresh in the moment.

At the heart of Baptiste Yoga are three themes; these are actions you can take and tools you can use to bring yourself back to center and begin again. They can help you deal with your distracted mind—your *monkey mind*, as it's often called. These are specific mental actions you can employ in the pose to disrupt the default drift of being in your head and quickly bring you back to center.

The first theme is *Be a Yes*. Right in the moment that you notice you've drifted off and tuned in to your mental chatter, re-embody the energy of YES.

Be a *yes* for making the higher call at each step.

Be a *yes* for triumph.

Be a *yes* for openness, for holding nothing back.

Be a *yes* for total acceptance of what is and what is not right now.

Be a *yes* for giving up resistance.

Be a *yes* for taking your attention off thoughts right now and grounding it in your physicality.

Be a *yes* for setting your eyes to one point out here in the physical environment.

Be a *yes* for moving a thunderous cleansing breath through your body.

Be a *yes* for putting your attention on your hands, your feet, your core, and activating muscle energy.

Be a *yes* for ease and flow.

Every time you get distracted or lulled into default resistance, remind yourself to be a *yes* for beginning again—to getting back to "out here" where life and real practice is actually happening.

The second theme is *Give Up What You Must*. Give up the stories you've made up about what's "true" about your physical potential and just be with your breath and in your body, feeling what you feel. Give up trying to collect things in your practice. Give up the thought that whatever is happening within your body right now should not be. Whatever you meet unexpectedly in the pose is not an interruption of the flow but rather a part of it. If it distracts and grabs you, simply give it up and begin again.

The third and final theme is *You Are Ready Now*. You are ready now to open yourself up. With kindness, allow yourself to begin again and again as many times as needed; the world and the pose will be experienced as much more friendly. Come from "I am ready now to awaken through everything that comes up in each moment." Come from "I am ready now to see all distractions as an invitation to bring meditation into the moment." If something does disrupt your drishti and flow and sweeps you off course, let it go and begin again. Come from "I am ready now to stay open and connect with the fresh, story-free presence of my body." If a negative narrative sneaks in, quickly give it up and begin again.

When you keep doing the work of bringing yourself back to true north, you get to look deep down and find out something profound about yourself. You come to know not just what you think or feel; you come to know yourself truly, profoundly, and deeply.

•

The greatest gift any teacher can receive is to see their words land in the hearts, minds, and bodies of their students. That is what happened for me on the day I encountered Brad, a yogi at one of my teacher-training workshops. His words are the best illustration I can offer of the art and promise of "begin again."

It was the third day of a weeklong program, and I was teaching Dancer's Pose. As the class of nearly 200 yogis held this elegant, one-legged balancing pose, I noticed quite a few people lacked ease and equanimity. It was as if their energy was stuck, and they were faltering and falling with a lot of visible frustration. I stopped the action in the room and requested that they all take a seat. For the next 10 minutes or so, we talked about the three themes of *Be a Yes, Give Up What You Must*, and *You Are Ready Now*, as I reminded them of the tools they had in their yogic toolbox. I asked if anyone had anything they wanted to share, and Brad raised his arm.

"Just now, I felt total frustration, because I kept falling out of the pose," he said. "I'm strong; I'm flexible; I know I can do this pose, but I felt distracted, and my balance sucked. The more I fell out of the pose, the more distracted I got. The whole experience made me feel frustrated, and eventually I got to this place of resignation, like 'If I can't do it perfectly, then I don't want to do it at all.'"

I reminded Brad—and the rest of the class—that the three themes jump right into the guts of unwanted attitudes, feelings, and disempowering mental scripts. They prompt you to take the one single action that is the way out of frustration and into flow: begin again.

I then asked Brad and the class to come back into Dancer's Pose, only this time with the slogan of "begin again" as their guide. I was not surprised to see an observable difference in the level of ease that was happening in the room.

After the pose was completed, I stopped the class once again to check in. Brad jumped up to his feet and was eager to share his experience the second time around: "I really listened to your words and it brought me into my body and into an experience of being totally clear. There was an experience of BIG SPACE . . . like I was peacefully hanging out in the gap between my thoughts. It was a moment of total astonishment and presence. In that clear space, I got deeply connected to my body in such a complete way. From my skin to my muscles to my bones, I was being held around the core of my torso in what felt like a unified muscle suit. I was in the most vividly connected EXPERIENCE of mind-body integration of my life and then WHAM . . . I started talking to myself again and it was over. Stuff like, *What do you think you're doing? You're not a 'be at peace in my body' kind of guy.* All my alignment and good feeling was gone and I fell out of the pose.

"In that moment, I breathed in the mantra of 'begin again,' and pretty much instantaneously, I was pulled back to my true north. I was a *yes* for it. I let go of my story about being 'Not that kind of guy' and was back in touch and out here with the pose, the practice, and what felt like all of life."

Through his on-the-mat experience, Brad discovered one of the essential truths about transformation. At all times and in all circumstances, you have the ability to powerfully shift the quality of your practice—no, make that your entire life—by the simple action of beginning again.

do the work

Do your practice and all is coming.

SRI K. PATTABHI JOIS

Many people come to yoga initially because they feel they have lost some connection with their body. Their body has aged or changed, or they may have had some type of health crisis that brought them to the realization that they've become "disembodied." That is to say, who they see themselves to be is not reflected in the body they inhabit.

Typically, when people take their first Baptiste–style yoga class, they quickly experience a gap between the concepts and beliefs they have about their bodies and what is actually happening in their physicality. Some believe they are stiff and discover they are far more flexible than they thought. Some think they are strong and are surprised that the strength they have acquired doing bench presses at the gym doesn't directly translate to strength on the mat. Others may believe they are completely lacking physically, only to discover they can do far more than they imagined.

Regardless of where you fall on the spectrum of disconnect, the first goal of the yogi is to re-enter your body. Part of that process is simply remembering that you have a body in the first place (which you may not have given thought to in a long time), and that it has treated you quite well, sometimes in spite of neglect or even abuse. The goal for the novice practitioner may not be to become a great yogi but rather to refocus their attention on their physical existence in space. This is what it means to *do the work* as a beginner.

Doing the work takes you out of wishing things to be different in your physicality or in your life and enables you to reap the greater rewards of yoga. You do the work on the mat and source that work from within yourself, and that allows for a fuller natural expression of your values, interests, and desires. Your work forms the asanas, which become the vehicle that activates your energy and sparks you back to life. On the surface, you are learning yoga practices and techniques, but underneath, you are intimately getting to know your own physical nature. Doing the work means bringing your mental theories, energy, and physical body together in harmony.

Yoga practice is distinct from most other personal growth methods because it comes from the premise that what you seek is already within you and won't be found by attaining some outer goal. Ultimately, it's a journey to the core of your own being. In the work of yoga, the outer point of the body is the doorway to access that which you are seeking within you. The work is to keep peeling away the layers of the onion to get to the heart of you.

There are many metaphors we can use for this. The lotus flower, for instance. The lotus flower is already there, hidden in the mud, obscured by the excess covering it. It doesn't need to be created or invented. The mud gets washed away, and suddenly there is the flower. The work to be done is to remove the layers that cover it. You don't have to add anything to your being; rather, you want to subtract and slough away some things. The work in that way is quite simple.

The question from there becomes: What steps do we need to take to do that work?

The original source of and creator of yoga, Patanjali, created eight steps, or "limbs," of yoga. They are:

1. Self-restraint (*yama*)
2. Fixed observance (*niyama*)
3. Posture (*asana*)
4. Breath control (*pranayama*)
5. Abstraction (*pratyahara*)
6. Concentration (*dharana*)
7. Meditation (*dhyana*)
8. Samadhi (*wholeness, with nothing lacking*)

These limbs are set out as steps because, just like climbing a ladder, there are levels, one after the next, that are the sequential path to elevated growth. Yoga offers us the steps of that ladder, and our job is to take each step and make the climb.

These steps are also referred to as the eight limbs of the tree of yoga. *Limbs* because they grow out of the uniqueness of the body's energy, and, just like your physical limbs, are applied to the individual's needs in the moment. These limbs are connected to the greater whole, and not necessarily linear. For example, my hands, feet, brain, and so on don't function separately from one another. They are organically connected, even though they perform separate functions. If my brain stops working, my hand or foot will stop moving because all the parts of my body are unified.

I always appreciated Patanjali's practicality in saying that we need both the linear steps and the organic application of the techniques in order to work holistically. You can put your attention on one step at a time, or on all of them, and that allows the limbs to grow organically, too. The linear steps and the more flowing, organic aspect of the limbs work together as a whole.

Mastery in yoga happens only when all eight limbs are discovered, embodied, and lived as a natural self-expression. But the work of yoga begins with the first three steps of *yama, niyama,* and *asana.* These give us our work and direction in the practice and take us out of wishing for physical transformation and into the action of creating it by our own energy and direction.

Yama is translated from Sanskrit to mean "self-restraint." But this English translation actually changes the meaning of the word *yama* as it is used in the context of yoga practice. Yama doesn't actually suggest constraint or repression in any way. The way Patanjali used the word meant to direct one's energy in ways that affirm life rather than waste or destroy that precious life force. Yama doesn't mean to repress your energy, but rather to direct it. Your habitual practices either direct your energy toward expansion and being a *yes*, or not.

The opposite of yama would be to have your energy traveling in a million different directions. It's the same energy—the same life force—only, without yama, it's scattered and thus diluted or even squandered. I've been in classes with newer teachers whose sequencing is overly creative because they are trying to impress the class or be entertaining, but as the student I'm left with the experience of moving all over the mat without real direction. It feels as though I'm moving uselessly, and that squandered energy creates frustration. This same kind of experience of having no direction can create the same kind of frustration in my life off the mat, as well. Without yama, we deplete our energy and are left with the experience of exhaustion without fulfillment.

Doing the work of creating self-restraint first requires that you give direction to your life energies. As we all know, our life energy has limits, and if you do not harness it, you cannot manifest all that's possible. Our life energy can be directed both on the mat and off in such a way that it becomes the doorway to limitless possibility.

Yama allows us to realize our innermost desires by directing our energy to fulfill them. On the mat and in life, you begin with yourself. To give direction to your desires and to move your energy in that direction means that you need to accept at the level of your bone marrow that you have free will and, therefore, responsibility for the direction you give your energy. We are all responsible for the actions we choose to take in the pose, and in life.

One of the three themes of Baptiste Yoga is *You Are Ready Now*. This means you begin with yourself, from within, and intentionally give direction to a pose. You create yama. Yama is the true north of your inner compass, moving you toward the thing you are a *yes* for.

In general terms, self-restraint on the mat means that you are becoming more centered by pulling in all the parts of your body toward centerline and integrating holistically into your body's core. From that core, you move your energy outward through your extremities in a beautiful, natural expression that brings you joy. You use yama when doing the work in a pose by being intentional, moving consciously, mobilizing and gathering your energies and expressing them with purpose, and orchestrating all your parts toward a unified direction.

True north alignment works much in the same way off the mat. Once you give direction to your life, and you are a *yes* for what you want to create, a deep sense of your own center immediately springs from within you. Direction (yama) creates the center, and then the center gives direction; both are mutually fulfilling in practice and in life.

Don't just wish for a direction. Instead, as if your whole life depended on it, do the work of getting clear for yourself what that direction is. That is the first step of yoga practice. It sets you up to take the second step up the ladder, which is *niyama*.

Niyama means "focused observance." This means that your life and practice have discipline and order to them. Niyama is the practice of regularity, but without rigidity. Unless you have a disciplined regularity in your practice, you will be left with just random impulses and instincts, and yama and asana will go out the window.

Sometimes people confuse discipline with "no freedom," but consider that discipline in the practice frees you from default thoughts and habits dominating your life. For instance, if you develop a discipline that you get on your mat every weekday morning for 30 minutes as soon as you awaken (or whatever your preferred routine looks like), then that habit becomes ingrained—you don't have to think about it. You don't have to constantly rearrange your schedule and juggle your priorities, because that's a set practice. If your yama is directed toward being a *yes* for your practice, then any default habits like, say, hitting the snooze button, have no space to take hold. Through discipline, you are given a freedom in body and being, a freedom to choose the direction of your life consciously and harness your energies to fulfill it. It is not a stretch to say that only the yogi who has regularity and discipline in his or her practice can hope to one day become a master.

The third step on the ladder is *asana*, which means "posture." The work to bring this step of yoga alive happens only by building off the first two steps. When you have the direction and the discipline—the regularity of getting on your mat—then you can cultivate powerful asana.

In every posture, the goal is to find the balance of effort and relaxation. Never restlessness. Whether in Wheel, Dancer's Pose, or seated in meditation, you want to create that balance. The novice yogi usually cannot sit still for 5 or 10 minutes in meditation without experiencing a total body restlessness and revolt. Typically, discomfort and pain of some kind arises in different points in the body, and the yogi resists or darts. When you sit still to meditate, however, you can get objective, measurable, and observable feedback on how far along you are in your yoga practice. If restlessness grabs hold, it's a signal that there has not been much practice of the first two steps of yama and niyama. Sitting still and relaxed in the seat of all postures is the true meaning of the word *asana*.

Doing the work in yoga practice means taking the steps and not skipping the ones you don't like. The limb of asana comes to life organically only to the yogi who does the work of organizing and purposefully directing their life energy and through a focused observance, which gives regularity; it is then that a whole world opens and a new kind of possibility emerges. Then you will notice, quite suddenly, that you can sit relaxed and still where in the past you could not, because your body now knows that you are a disciplined person. If you want to sit still in meditation, you will, because your body has been trained not to resist that. You can sit not because you are lucky, or particularly laid-back, but because you did the work. Your body will know what it is to relax and be at ease, where before it knew only restlessness. When you can be relaxed, the stress of life drops away.

●

There are three elements we must ground ourselves in when doing the work. The first is our capacity to awaken (and reawaken) our idealism. The second is our ability to be intimate in how we interact with our poses and practice. And the third is our willingness to choose depth in the face of the ever-quickening pace of modern life.

The culture we live in has forsaken idealism for cynicism, sold out intimacy for consumption, and sacrificed depth for speed. As a result, we find ourselves disconnected and disembodied. When we lose idealism, intimacy, and depth in our work on the mat, we end up doing poses purely on a cosmetic level, pushed along the modern-day yogic conveyor belt of "mastery" and motivated by outward forms and appearances. We fall out of touch with our center and act as if we are at the effect of our practice, rather than its cause.

There is a compelling tendency among novice practitioners and teachers developing their skills to quickly race past the fundamentals and move on to more elaborate and sophisticated poses, practices, or techniques. Understandably, novice yogis love to demonstrate risk, cleverness, and originality in poses and sequences, probably because they can be dramatic, fun, and awe-inspiring—especially in a room full of eager yogis.

This is the novice yogi's curse, however, be they a new student or a new teacher. The curse is manifested as a practice laced with frivolous adornment and weak fundamentals. It is marked by a lack of depth and intimacy, and, ultimately, delayed mastery. If you have ever had the opportunity to be taught by a true master of yoga—or of any discipline, really—you have likely been struck by how simple and fundamental the instruction was. Stripped of pretense, it is grounded in what truly matters. A true master knows that wisdom is both beautiful and powerful in its simplicity.

From time to time when traveling, I drop in to yoga classes in different cities, and rarely these days do I see taught the fundamental and essential principles of Tadasana—the physical pose of whole-body integration that, when created consciously, embodies true north alignment. Asana is present, but yama and niyama are missing, and so the depth is naturally absent.

It is natural for teachers to want to teach fancy poses. The urge to quickly move away from the basics (and after all, what can be more basic than Tadasana?) and toward advanced movements arises out of the natural desire to impress students with one's skills and knowledge. But make no mistake: it is a novice teacher who does that. Teaching a tripod headstand where there is not yet a classical headstand, or teaching a standing drop-back into Wheel Pose where there is not yet a firm grasp of shoulder and pelvic integration is a colossal mistake. This rush to advancement puts you, and the student, at risk for injury. It also delays your honest advancement and glosses over the deeper body work that would give depth to the movement. In short, it stunts your practice.

On the other hand, if the instructor insists on the basics—really insists on them—you will immediately recognize that you are learning from a master teacher. The most effective teachers do the least amount of teaching, and allow you to discover things for yourself. You will not be bored or overwhelmed; you will be inspired. I promise this will always be true. When taught effectively, you will quickly come to recognize the power and potency of your fundamentals of true north alignment, breath, flow, and drishti. You will advance in every measurable way, past those not blessed to have a teacher grounded and committed to the basics.

So what do you, as the student, do when you find yourself on your mat, being taught by a teacher who does not bring the *yama* and *niyama* to his or her teaching? You bring it yourself, to your own practice. You bring the commitment to directing your energy to whatever you are a *yes* for. You bring the focused observance—the discipline. You bring in true north alignment, breath, flow, and drishti to each pose in your practice. Come from a place of surrender and trust in yourself, and have faith in your own capacities.

the myth of
the real yogi

The privilege of a lifetime is being who you are.

JOSEPH CAMPBELL

What is a real yogi?

When I ask my students in teacher trainings this question, here's what they say:

A real yogi is . . .

Serene
Peaceful
Compassionate
Open
Embracing
Loving
Patient

Kind
Vegetarian
Fit
Flexible
Enlightened

A "real yogi" conceals their imperfections. They hide the fact that they're messy, that they lose their patience with their kids or curse when they get stuck in traffic, that they eat pizza. A "real yogi" certainly never lets others see they are flawed, and says things like "I accept you" and, of course, "Namaste."

But to me, real yogis are not defined by these things. Sure, they may embody some of these qualities, but more often than not, one who is striving to be a "real yogi" is hiding behind that persona. The problem with the myth of the real yogi is that it ends up being a mask that keeps us separated from who we truly are and, very often, the things we want most in life. It leaves us with the sensation of being not quite comfortable in our own skin and robs us of authentic confidence and genuine, heart-to-heart relationships.

I've been around the yoga world long enough to be fluent in the language I call *yoga-nese*. You know: that flowery peace, love, and granola compassion stuff that is almost always a big facade. Believe me, I've seen some pretty shocking stuff under those facades! These people are like pirate ships waving the white peace flag, all conciliatory, but then, if you accidentally cross them, WHOOSH . . . out come the mental swords and verbal daggers and before you know it, you're walking the emotional gangplank.

I see a real yogi as someone who is committed to growth and to being the best version of themselves, and, at the same time, is courageous enough to be fully present and authentic in each moment. Someone who is not afraid to get real about the whole mess of who they are—the good, the bad, and the ugly; someone who can be open and own that they get depressed, stressed out, pissed off; that they sometimes yell at their spouse; that they watch television, drink coffee, eat bacon. Please don't misunderstand: I'm not advocating that anyone be any specific way. It's just important to acknowledge who we are in all our forms and personal expressions, even if sometimes those forms are not how we'd like ourselves to be.

Why? Because hiding behind a mask costs us so much and leaves us with so little. On the surface, we may look polished and "perfect," but hiding our true self in all its dimensions saps our life energy and robs us of the freedom to express ourselves genuinely, from the heart. Hiding leaves you with the experience of feeling splintered and having lost yourself. You can have the fabulous yoga outfit; know the name of every pose in Sanskrit; and even have a beautiful, super-flexible, strong practice. But the real question to ask is "Where are *you* in all of that?" And, even more, "What is hiding behind all those trappings costing you?"

So many of us hide. We hide behind our accomplishments, our degrees, our bank balance, our carefully cultivated public personas. Greg, a student of mine who came to a teacher training in upstate New York, shared his experience of hiding that I think hits home for so many people. Greg is a highly successful executive who runs a well-known tech company. By his own description, he has a beautiful wife, three wonderful kids, a big house, lots of friends, and enough money to never have to work another day in his life if he chooses. In his community as well as at work, he's known as someone who gets things done. On the surface, by Greg's own admission, his life looks perfect.

Underneath all that, though (no surprise), Greg is a mess. He has every symptom of stress you can imagine: stomach problems, anxiety, insomnia, and more. Though he appreciates all the comforts he has, he feels like a slave to his lifestyle and the persona he's created. As he put it, "I put one hundred percent of my energy into keeping all the balls up in the air, making sure that everyone thinks well of me. But I'm exhausted. Sometimes I look at my beautiful wife and kids and have the sense of missing them, even when they're right next to me. I've lost sense of what matters to me . . . what I like to do."

I asked Greg: "So what is all this hiding costing you?"

Without missing a beat, he responded, "The life I actually want. Love. Connection. Joy. Freedom. But no more. I realized right this second that I want those things much more than anything my lifestyle can give me."

As he said those words, every single one of us in the room (and I mean myself, 10 of my staff, and 250 other yogis) witnessed his entire energy transform right in front of our eyes. The heaviness dissipated from his body and lifted from his face as he relaxed into the lightness, brightness, and ease that comes from dropping the mask, opening the heart, and being oneself.

There's no fulfillment in looking the part or talking the talk—in real life or in yoga practice. So forget being a "real yogi" and just be the yogi you are. Be simple, open, and straightforward about what matters to you and what you are working on. The true reward of yoga practice comes when we are courageous enough to step out from behind that mask and expose our brilliant, flawed, utterly human selves. No covering up, no apologizing—just taking responsibility for it all.

If there are things you don't like about the yogi that you are, that's okay. Owning them frees you to do the work to change those things. Being straight up with yourself about where you are being inauthentic creates an opening to direct your life energies toward what calls to you in your heart. Being open instead of closed is a way for you to discover your potential. Whenever you follow your potential you align to your true north, which energetically supports you in what you are up to in your life and practice. Whenever you go back into hiding and pretending, you go astray from your potential. You experience yourself shrinking for the simple reason that you are not being who you are destined to be, and who it is possible for you to be. You are being something else and thus experience the hollowness that comes from being someone you are not.

Embrace the naked truth of who and where you are in your practice and in your life. Hiding is secure, but life is about insecurity. Nothing is guaranteed. If your yoga is about really living fully, then you have to live at risk and in the danger that comes with being your open-book self. If you want to climb the highest peaks, then you have to take the risk of falling from somewhere, and perhaps the place to risk falling is from where you are right now. The pathway to authenticity demands courage, and with courage you can go to the places that scare you and risk falling down—although you will most likely surprise yourself and fly.

the cosmic joke

*The only person you are destined to
become is the person you decide to be.*

RALPH WALDO EMERSON

We all live under the influence of a great cosmic joke, and it goes something like this:

At some point in your life—most likely when you were young—you came to believe something about yourself. Someone said something to or about you, or something happened, and you took it to mean that you were limited in some way, or flawed, or compromised. Without you even realizing it, one small event became the defining theme of your life.

Here's how it happens:

Let's imagine you got separated from your parents at a big sports arena. You looked around and suddenly, no one you knew was there with you. Though you

119

didn't know it consciously at the time, that experience got emotionally rooted in you and you made it mean *I'm all alone in the world.*

A kid told you in first grade that you're stupid, and you bought into that. Since then, you've lived your whole life believing that you're not smart enough to accomplish your goals.

You were abandoned, hurt, or harmed in other ways by someone, and you took that as proof that you're not lovable. And ever since, that belief has driven your actions and decisions. You've believed you're not worthy of love, so perhaps you've left relationship after relationship, looking for the one that fulfills you.

You've believed you're not worthy, so you over-achieve to disprove that to yourself. Yet no matter what you accomplish, you never quite feel happy. You're the best in your work, as a parent, on your yoga mat, but still your perception of yourself deep down doesn't change.

Ready for the joke of it? That belief on which you've based your entire life *is not real.* You made it up. Or someone said it to you and you took their opinion as absolute fact.

You made up that you're not strong . . . that you're not lovable . . . that you're not important . . . that

nothing ever works out for you . . . that money is evil
. . . that if you try something new, you'll look foolish.

But these beliefs are not the truth.

The truth is not that you're unlovable; it's that you
made up that you're not lovable.

The truth is not that you're weak; it's that you
made up that you're not strong.

The truth is not that you're alone in the world; it's
that you made up that no one supports or cares for you.

And yet every action you've taken, every word
you've said, every decision you've made, every relationship you've formed or ended, every opportunity
you've taken or shied away from has been dictated
by that wrong assumption you've come to think of as
"The Truth about Me."

If your first reaction to hearing this is something
like, "Wait a minute, Baron. I understand that this
might be true for others, and I can see how they make
stuff up about themselves, but that's not me," then I
invite you to pause here for a moment. Stop, take a
deep breath, find your feet, find your seat, and take
a deeper look at your life. Look beyond the surface
experiences and ask yourself if perhaps, just maybe,
your beliefs have been running the show. We believe
life happens to us, but so much of it we create by our
own hand. How much of what's occurred in your life

repeats or has a consistent theme? There is usually the most obvious place to look for how and where the cosmic joke is at play in your life.

You've been a walking reaction to something you made up when you were 5, 10, 15 years old. But you're reacting to ghosts . . . to stuff that isn't even here today, and that's exhausting. If you're not responding to what's actually happening right here, but rather reacting to your thoughts about what's right here, you're trapped in it. You keep doing, doing, doing—trying to get someplace new, but you keep landing back in the same place. Nothing gets better in our lives as long as we're trying to outsmart the joke. You'll move the pieces around—change jobs, cities, relationships, even yoga styles—but the joke follows you. You've heard the Zen saying "Wherever you go, there you are."

Here's where the joke gets even more absurd: We make stuff up about things that didn't even happen yet. We project our default belief into every situation, and before we have to feel that feeling, we just take ourselves out. *Oh, this person will leave me, so I'm not even going to get involved . . . I won't be able to do that pose or class, so I won't even try . . . Meditation might be great for some people, but it won't work for me, so why bother?*

Here's a question to consider: How much of what's happening in your head has to do with what's happening in life, right here? My guess is absolutely nothing. Think about that. Your belief that you're not strong literally has no bearing on your ability to do Crow Pose, other than to throw up resistance to your trying. Your body can objectively do what it can do, regardless of what you believe. That's the joke of it!

Seeing all of this could make you want to cry, but allowing for the enormity of it is actually a good thing. Though it can seem deeply sobering and heavy just before you get the humor of the joke, please don't bother running a whole number on yourself for falling for it; that's just another way to keep yourself trapped in the vicious loop. Step back and look at it from the observer perspective, and just like getting the punch line of any joke, you will suddenly be struck with the aha moment. You may not know whether to laugh or cry at first, seeing how much this false belief has run your life. But it'll take you much further to lighten up and laugh at the ridiculousness of it, and instead focus on the good news, which is this:

You had the power to make up this limiting belief, and you can use that same power to un-make it. When you see your default in the clear light of day, you're no longer in its grip. You've stepped into the space where you have freedom of choice, in which you can decide to fall back into its grip and get more of the same, or do something new.

•

Asana practice is a rich opportunity to unearth our thoughts and move forward into a life free of those confining beliefs. The practice clears out old energy, creating new space. As we go through the flow of poses, things get energetically stirred up, which can be confronting. With experience, we get skillful at allowing the practice to work on us. We hold a space that allows for whatever needs to come up to do so, and we let it go.

Let's say I'm holding Pigeon Pose, feeling an uncomfortable physical sensation. And let's also say I have a belief I've made up or bought into that I am not strong enough to weather difficulty. As soon as the physical discomfort kicks in, so, too, will my default belief to signal the alarm bells of *I can't do this, get the heck out of here!* Certainly, I can cut bait and come out of the pose. Or, I can allow that thought to come up, feel what I need to feel, give it up, and stay. I can get curious about what will happen to me if I just stay and be with my experience instead of running. By staying, I would discover that old emotional energy rises up and, if I just watch it, it will evaporate. Maybe I'd need to make appropriate physical shifts in the moment to adapt the physical pose, but the energetic debris would dissolve away.

My father had such depth to what he taught, but as a kid I never really understood what he was talking about. I remember when I was 10 years old being in my father's meditation class at my parents' yoga center in San Francisco. My father said to the class something to the effect of, "As you sit there dealing with your own mind, remember this: when interacting with thoughts in your head, or when interacting with another person in life, and something is thought or said to you that upsets you and makes you want to fight or flee, wait twenty-four hours before you respond."

At the time I didn't get what he was talking about. But now I do. If some thought in my head agitates or upsets me, or someone says something that insults me, I will first respond by saying to myself, "I will come back to my mat after twenty-four hours have passed, and determine then how or if I want to respond to the upsetting thought or insult. Even if the upsetting thought came from me and was something about my own practice." This practice has opened up a whole new world in my own practice and continues to do so to this day.

A response is different than a reaction. A reaction is automatic—out of default—and a response is conscious. On the mat and off, it happens like this: some default thought arises, and if you immediately react to that thought, then you resist or quit, and there is not a single gap of time and space to get any perspective. You're trapped in pure reaction. Or you can wait and see, and get curious about what else might arise. That allows space for conscious response rather than automatic reaction. Patience has been a powerful thing for me to develop, and the approach of waiting has taught me to see the "gaps" as points of power. There is a power of release that's given by letting things just be.

Asana practice empowers us to experience the joyful free space on the other side of all the disempowering beliefs—what the yogis call *samadhi*. The word *samadhi* has beautiful depth of meaning. On one level, it means to see through a clear lens. But beyond that, samadhi refers to the "space," which is the place from which the yogi observes. In this context, samadhi means everything is resolved: there is no "beyond" place to arrive to that will make you happier. This is it. Everything, including you, is whole, complete, and lacking nothing. In other words, you have come home.

What if instead of coming from disempowering beliefs you came from samadhi, your true north center, in every pose and danced in the pose from a place of already being at home with it all? You got the joke and now from samadhi you are free to be in the pose and create whatever you want in contrast to trying to fix something or get it right. Imagine how that would be . . . what you could do . . . what would be possible for you.

Once you get the cosmic joke, you naturally use everything in your life to lighten up rather than adding heaviness to your experience. If you do get swept up and spin off into seriousness, significance, and heaviness, choose to give it up and send it out on the outbreath. If you can practice this in the face of all that comes up, then you are well trained. Being well trained means that living inside the cosmic joke is over, because you can catch yourself when the disempowering belief looms and lighten up to let it go. You can use everything that comes up as a way to bring yourself back to the present moment, just like when you are about to fall out of a balance pose and catch yourself before you do and recover center.

What if you've read all this and still don't get the joke? Let's say it's over your head and under your heels, and you really don't get what I'm talking about, much like I didn't get what my father meant at first all those years ago. That's okay. Here's a tip: just remember that doing anything that begins to shift the pattern and lessen the gravity of suffering or frustration is a breakthrough. In each pose and in every practice you undertake in your life, cultivate a practice of lightening up and not taking so seriously the failures and successes, the rewards and the consequences.

Great freedom arises from the experience of lightness.

Learn to laugh at the ridiculousness of the great cosmic joke. If you can practice lightening up even when taking yourself seriously, you will know you are up to something bigger in your practice and your life.

strive not to arrive

There is no end to education. It is not that you read a book, pass an examination, and finish with education. The whole of life, from the moment you are born to the moment you die, is a process of learning.

KRISHNAMURTI

I often hear students say they want to "get Handstand" or "get Crow Pose." Certainly, that kind of intention is powerful, because it gives you something to grow into. And, at the same time, there's really no such thing as "getting" a pose. With regular practice and by learning the tools and techniques, you can attain the physical form of a pose, and that kind of achievement is invigorating. But mastery of form isn't the ultimate goal. Just doing more, better, or different poses is not the endgame; full revelation of your humanity and aliveness is.

It doesn't matter how beautifully you do a posture or how flexible your body is; if you do not have the unification of the body, the mind, and the breath, it is difficult to say that your practice falls into the definition of yoga. After all, yoga is an inner experience through which your entire being is touched and moved. It includes external form but is not limited to just that.

Asanas are useful tools to align the body, mind, emotions, and breath, but you want to give up the idea that they are projects to be completed and achieved and begin to see them as doorways opening into greater discovery and action that will take you into being more fully alive. A carpenter uses tools to build something that brings forth some intended result. If the focus becomes *how to* use the tools instead of *why* use the tools, the big picture gets lost.

Similar to how a yogi uses asana, the Zen masters use archery. They practice taking concentrated aim with eye and body in coordination, again and again until they master hitting the bull's-eye. When they reach the skill level that allows for hitting the bull's-eye every time, they throw away the bow and arrow—the "form" that gave them access to that level of embodied discovery. They no longer need it, as they have successfully used the bow and arrow to manifest intention into reality and hone their powers of concentration, which are now an embodied part of who they are.

Just like the Zen masters, you want to look beyond form and the surface performance. Consider that the goal of the practice surpasses mastery of the pose and its form. Asanas offer the opportunity to realize the greater goal of yoga, which is hidden deep inside the pose. You cannot find it on the surface; you will have to exceed yourself to penetrate to the very center of it.

Mastery is never about arrival. It is fluid, not fixed, and always about the continuing journey. One of the most fundamental things to remember in yoga practice is your life and practice must gain depth in order to expand and transcend itself. Beyond mastery of form is the possibility of substance. If you don't embrace this and instead think you've "arrived," then you will be lost in the dullness of the "how to" and will not see all the new possibilities organically arising around you. The forms of the poses are a means to an end. They are not the end in and of themselves, because there is no end.

The yogi always starts out as a form junkie. We all have our own attachment to creating strong, beautiful poses, and we bring this attachment onto the mat. We become attached to what the practice looks like and forget that it is an opportunity to understand something deeper—something far more extraordinary than having a perfectly balanced Eagle Pose. Nothing is wrong with mastering form, but the bigger work for each of us is to have a transformation not in our poses, but in our internal paradigm.

It's great for us to be able to measure our strength, flexibility, stamina, and overall progress in the pose, and attention to form allows for that. The problem, however, is that usually we don't just measure the progress or condition we're dealing with in the pose; we make that measure mean something about who we are as human beings. If the form of the pose gets labeled as "good" by some standard, then I am good. If it is "not good," then I am no good, either. If the form is not enough, I make that mean that I am not enough. Rather than saying, "My leg muscles are not strong enough to sustain this pose," one might say, "I am not strong enough to hold this pose." Can you see the difference? One is a measure of leg strength; the other is a measure of who you are as a human being.

The way we attempt to fix being "not enough" is to acquire more technical knowledge, try harder, seek to understand it better. All these are useful strategies in their own right, but also ones that leave us working the pose from only one paradigm. A focus on form lets us feel in control and gives us something measurable to strive for. It's tempting to seek quick action and quick results. Whether we admit it to ourselves or not, most of us are addicted to being in control. It's how we survive the pose, the class, the job, the marriage, life: by seeking to get it under our control.

Misplaced hope is the expectation that some external source is going to save or legitimize us, so we can eventually live happily ever after. It is a superstitious belief that if we master the right form (on or off the mat), we will someday "arrive."

If we think of a "form" as anything we do and the things we have, we can see that's true. A relationship that looks a certain way is a form. So, too, is a large bank account, the perfect physique, an award won or a promotion granted. Yet in the background of our consciousness, we have all experienced enough disappointment with the ability of forms to deliver true fulfillment. Hoping that we will "arrive" in contentment when we achieve these things keeps all the suffering in place.

In this paradigm, we see our well-being as completely dependent on something external. All this leads to disillusionment because, ultimately, no form of activity or acquisition, on or off the mat, can deliver what we hope it can. A slightly more extended Dancer's Pose can never satisfy the hunger in one's heart.

Transforming our experience of our practice requires that we stop believing that more, better, different poses will give us something they simply cannot. That does not mean that a focus on form has no value, or that we need to give it all up and just flop around on our mats like wet noodles. We simply need to recognize the place form has in our practice, and take a stand for not allowing it to be a measure of who or how we are as practitioners.

Of course, we want to perform the poses with a focus on intelligent mechanics of body movement, creating energetic efficiency, along with appropriate intensity of action, and push ourselves to the point of discomfort in order to create new results. But, at the same time, we want to be detached from insatiably perfecting that form and instead seek and create a depth of experience.

If we look deeper and stop expecting anything outside of ourselves to fulfill us, we experience a fundamental shift in our relationship to ourselves and our practice. We get committed first to our own well-being and less to a concern for looking good, getting it right, or arriving at the right answer. We begin to choose depth and quality of experience instead of avoiding unpleasant emotions and feelings. We engage in the inquiry of "Is what I am doing going to serve my dignity and vitality? Is it empowering depth and substance, or is it avoiding something by focusing only on form?" We begin to make choices in each moment, pose to pose, breath to breath, that are based on the essence of our experience and a bigger, deeper discovery of possibility.

I was participating in a class being given by my teacher, Mr. Iyengar. In his booming voice, he instructed the class to "Go beyond the limitations of the mind" in the poses. He went on to say, "The moment you think you've arrived, you get squashed like a bug."

Mr. Iyengar then instructed us to do Rajakapotasana (King Pigeon Pose). *I've got this,* I thought, as I bent my back knee and brought my foot up toward the back of my head, grabbing it with both hands. I pulled my foot to my head into an ever-deeper backbend.

Half of my consciousness was with my body, applying technical skills and mechanics to properly create
the physical pose. The other half was with my ego as I
"performed" the pose. The practice room was very full
that day, and I remember being aware of how other
yogis in the room were watching me. I was also aware
that my teacher and his senior assistants were watching me as well. So, with my concern for looking good
in full throttle, I kept pulling with each breath deeper
and deeper into the full form of this backbend. Suddenly, POP . . . I felt my lower back give out as a shoot-
ing pain radiated from my hip to my spine.

As I slowly came out of the pose, Mr Iyengar's next
words rang out loudly like a bell ringing in my head:
"The mind is a friend or it is a foe." In that moment,
I saw with a flash that the part of my mind that was
attached to mastering form had been driving me impa-
tiently toward seeking quick results; depth and substance were nowhere to be found in my expression. My
rush to perform the pose in my teacher's class left me
injured, and my whole physical practice screeched to
a halt for a while after that. That day was a paradigm-
altering experience for me, and a great reminder that
an over-focus on form and results comes with a cost.

There is a Zen saying: "If you are in a hurry, you
will never reach your goal." After that experience of

being injured, I got clear that when I choose to slow down and deepen my experience on the mat, I open up to a bigger kind of thinking and profound learning. The less I'm in a hurry, the quicker the results seem to happen. With patience, the quality of my experience has a depth that can't be measured on the clock, but by the timelessness of my experience. We fool ourselves when we ask how long it will take to get the pose, to know who we are, or figure out our life purpose.

It's reasonable to think at first that "slowing down" means to move through the forms of the poses more slowly. But do you really think you would access your humanity by the pace of your moves on the mat? That's like saying that someone who runs has less ability to be meditative than someone who walks. Slowing down your tempo might help you work on your body mechanics and form, but that is still looking to the form to fix something. The real work here is to slow down and create space within yourself. It is very meaningful to be in the pose and let the experience of it penetrate you deeply. Letting the pose work on us requires patience.

Yoga practice forces us to confront our impatience; we learn over time the more impatient we are, the more time it will take for us to reach our transformation. It's counterintuitive, but the more we are in a hurry the more our growth will be delayed. The yogis say the moment you are infinitely patient is the moment that you allow for a transformation.

The true face of mastery is ease and depth. Watching Mr. Iyengar perform poses would often remind me of an elite athlete or premier dancer on stage. It was as if he would enter another dimension—"the zone"—in which he could make the difficult and even the supernatural seem effortless. He moved through asanas like an artist at play with a creative force, his essence being expressed through his movements and accessing something way beyond the limitations of simply achieving some physical form.

When we think we've "arrived," it is typically because we think we understand something. We know it and can handle it. But as Mr. Iyengar showed through his own practice, when you have mastered something, instead of you doing it, it does you.

All great teachers are perpetual students. There is always more to learn, more to explore, more to discover. I believe when Mr. Iyengar said, "The minute you think you've arrived, you get squashed like a bug," he meant that your growth is halted. The instant you become filled up with your know-how, you hit a dead end. As soon as you believe you've mastered form or have arrived, you give up learning.

To continue to grow and expand, you must be malleable. And to be malleable is to be teachable. Part of being teachable means being open and allowing the teacher's words to land in your body. So often, when a teacher begins speaking, we go into default and immediately think, *Oh, I know what he's going to say.* Or worse, as soon as they call the pose, we tune out the teacher entirely, drop into default, and go on autopilot. But you showed up on your mat as a student; why not open yourself up, get curious, and perhaps learn something new?

You all know a lot. You've studied, read, traveled, experienced, researched, and survived much. I acknowledge and applaud every ounce of wisdom you've collected along the way. At the same time, you've likely heard the phrase "Yesterday's breakthrough is today's ego trip." Consider that you did all of that so you can most powerfully face—with open eyes, open ears, and an open heart—what's up for you right here, in this moment. All your hard work on the mat and off has led you to this moment, when you are being called to let it all go and make space for new insights and experiences.

When you achieve the physical skill and capacity to take any form in the way you are striving for, there's always another level of discovery available to you. That's where the invaluable process of inquiry comes in. Ask yourself: *What crossroad do I find myself in at this point in my practice?* This question affirms that it is the complexity of the practice that gives it deeper meaning. The fact that we can acknowledge we are at a crossroad gives us the energy to get through it. This intersection represents an unfulfilled desire to change our direction, and shows us what we want to put our attention on and what we want to take it off.

Ask, *What do I want to create for myself in my practice? What commitment am I willing to make to make that happen?* If change and growth are to happen, they will come from your own free choice and demand the essential investment of personal commitment.

Lastly, what is the question that if you had the answer would set you totally free? Each time you ask and answer this question, you will find it takes you in a different direction. There may not be one answer to it, but each answer will illuminate the path to what's next for you.

The Buddha talks about how the wheel of life keeps on moving, and how the wheel turns around a fixed center. If you look only at the periphery of the wheel, you are looking at the outer form. If you become capable of accessing the hub, the core center, you will be able to connect with something essential, timeless, and eternal. When we focus on form and look only to the periphery, we find ourselves repeating the same superficial motions again and again and again.

Buddha calls life a wheel because things go on habitually repeating themselves. The more you mechanically repeat the same form of the poses, the sooner your practice will go flat as boredom and dullness sets in. If you've been on the mat for enough hours in your life, you've probably hit that kind of rut in your practice at one time or another, likely without realizing why. A singular focus on form robs you of freshness and creativity, and the practice quickly grows stale. Buddha calls this unconscious repetitious turning of the wheel *samsara*. Outside of this repetitious rut is where you will discover nirvana.

When I was in my early twenties living in Los Angeles, I would attend an early morning open class every day at a local studio where yogis would gather and go through a set sequence of postures, each at his or her own pace. Day in and day out, I would notice that some of the yogis seemed to be just going through the motions. They would repeat the forms of the practice again and again, with technical acumen but with no spark in their eyes and no rays of energy expressing out from the center of the pose. There was a mechanical dullness in what they were doing. In observing them, I realized that I, too, had the ability to go unconscious and robotically move through the forms.

What I discovered for myself was that the moment I feel that I've "arrived" because I've mastered some form is when I fall into that realm of the repetitive robotic rut of dullness. I learned that to keep expanding, I need not to get caught up in the periphery pursuits and instead reach deeper and get to the source of my experience.

Vinyasa—the flow from pose to pose—is a moving wheel on an unmoving hub at the center. You are the hub. The outer flow of the wheel keeps on moving, taking you someplace new. Why strive to "arrive" when that would mean the wheel of knowledge, inspiration, depth, and discovery would come to a halt?

complete with heart

We will be more successful in all our endeavors if we can let go of the habit of running all the time, and take little pauses to relax and re-center ourselves. And we'll also have a lot more joy in living.

THICH NHAT HANH

And . . . Savasana.

Those magic words spoken by the teacher at the end of class can be a huge relief! Finally, after all your hard work on your mat today, comes a chance to rest deeply and let go of doing and trying. Indeed, Savasana does promise deep rest, but that is far from the beginning and end of what it offers us.

As a pose, Savasana is unique. Its promise is simple and straightforward: you allow it to be, and it allows you to be.

The essence of Savasana can be summed up in three short sentences:

Here is where it is.
Now is when it is.
You are what it is.

In other words, if we allow it to be so, Savasana is the purest expression of full presence. It allows us to expand through simply *being,* without any trying, thinking, or effort required.

How often in life do we get a gift as sweet as that?

I realize that when asking a class to take Savasana—to really do nothing and just be and relax with what is—I am asking them to do something that is not always easy. For some, it may occur as uncomfortable, or even threatening. It takes courage to just be with yourself instead of humming along with your favorite playlist.

Savasana is the completing pose of yoga practice. It is an opportunity to come home to yourself—where you can see that there really is no "home" unless you find it within yourself. It is the place where your whole being is awakened, where you allow and accept all feelings and emotions to arise—comfortable or otherwise. It's where we learn that openness is the key to inner strength and that it doesn't come from resisting our fears and feelings, but rather from allowing them to rise up and then letting them go. It is the place to simply be you, simply and fully as you are.

Ordinarily on the mat, we do poses as a way of becoming something more: better, wiser, stronger, greater. Through our efforts and actions, we are embodying the energy of "becoming," which is distinct from just "being." In Savasana, we discover the possibility of just being. No trying, no effort. Savasana is the practice of non-action—non-doing—and that is the space of being.

Each of us has experienced those magic moments in life of pure being, when we're fully present and engaged in the moment. Whether these moments in life are frequent or rare, in Savasana, we can get in touch with that place within ourselves as a conscious act and access it at will.

•

Baptiste Yoga is centered around three embodied themes: *Be a yes; Give up what you must*; and come from *You are ready now*. These themes are valuable tools in every pose, but in Savasana they move from being tools to becoming embodied in who you are.

As you surrender to the completing pose, be a yes for openness. Be a yes for being yourself. Be a yes for giving yourself over to something greater, to allowing for something new, to holding nothing back. Be a yes for the rising and falling of your chest with each breath, for that natural ebb and flow of life force in and out of your body.

Drop into your body and give up any need to exert effort, to control, achieve, or accomplish. Give up any "shoulds." Give up your to-do list. Give up any remaining resistance. Give it all up to get empty.

Come from a place of *I am ready now to surrender and relax with what is.*

Allow all of what you've done up to this point on your mat to seep in and be fully received in your body, mind, and being. You are ready now to root down deeper and expand your energetic space upward and outward.

Like meditation, Savasana holds the space for powerful breakthroughs. A student named Wendy once shared this breakthrough—one of thousands I've been privileged to witness:

"In Savasana today," she said, "I saw how much I get disempowered by worry. I'm always worrying about what I should be doing; I even worry about what I'm not doing. Even while I'm doing what I think I should be doing, I worry that I'm not doing it right. As I was lying there today, I was actually worrying that I wasn't 'doing' Savasana right, and I realized I have a choice: I can keep worrying about what I should be doing or that I should be doing something better or different, or I can let go of all that and allow myself the gift of acceptance. In that moment, everything in me got calm and peaceful, and for the first time I can remember, I felt totally free in myself. I could just be."

She continued, "I now see that Savasana is an opportunity, like you said, to fully accept that *this is it*, and there is nothing to fix, make right, or figure out. Savasana isn't the end of my practice. It's actually a new beginning."

As Wendy saw, empowerment in Savasana for any of us requires that we have a breakthrough in acceptance. It calls for an internal shift from "doing nothing can't be it" to accepting "this is it." As you lie still, you come to experience that all is imperfectly perfect, just as it is. You accept where you are and where you are not, as you are and as you are not. In this space of Savasana arises the strength and freedom to choose what is and is not, exactly as it is, and to choose how you will act (or not act) going forward, both on and off the mat.

Like so many yogis I've known, I have personally had a transformative experience in Savasana. In a single moment, from nothing and out of nowhere, I had a paradigm shift. After that moment, my body and my circumstances were all the same, but I was not. As the observer of myself and my life, I saw my entire existence and practice in a whole new light.

In Sanskrit, *sava* means "death," and *asana* means "seat." In this particular Savasana on that day, I was confronted with my own experience of walking through the valley of the shadow of death.

It happened at the end of a not particularly extraordinary yoga practice; there was nothing significant about my being on my mat that day in the Baptiste Yoga Center in Cambridge, Mass. But there I was, on my back on my mat, when I had the realization that everything my life had been about up to that point was meaningless and empty. I saw, with a jolt, that the things I thought were so significant—like looking good, by being a well-known teacher, and spreading the lofty practice of yoga—meant nothing.

At the time, I was dealing with struggles in my marriage and with a business partner, and a travel schedule that kept me away from my kids, and I came face-to-face with a feeling of being massively thwarted and a total sense of hopelessness. I had a profound sense that I was alone and not good enough, smart enough, strong enough to deal with all of the commitments and complexities of my life. In that moment, my life occurred to me as stuck, impossible, and bleak; I was left with the feeling that I had nothing to offer, nothing to draw on. No help, no way out. (You see now why I refer to this experience as walking through the valley of the shadow of death).

Then, right there in Savasana, I just let go of all trying and all doing. I dropped every muscle and bone into the firm floor and sank into the ground of my being. As I truly released everything, it was as if something released me. Something let go, and all of a sudden, there was "no-thing" between me and the pulse beating in my chest. Something lifted, and it was as if I was elevated above the battlefield of my mind. All the heaviness in my body and being vanished.

That was when I was hit with the realization that all I had been struggling with and all I had accomplished was without real significance. It had no inherent meaning other than the meaning assigned to it all. In my body, I felt fully alive and awake, with both profound sadness and gladness, anguish and peace in my heart. On the one hand, I was saddened that I'd wasted my life up until that point in needless contention with others, thinking I was somehow special or important because of things I'd accomplished.

And right along with that realization swiftly came another: *Wow, I'm free.* My life suddenly occurred to me as an unwritten, open book that I was free to author a different way. From that day forward, I was free to create my life as something bigger than just myself and my concerns. That was a soul-altering experience for me into the greater purpose of my life.

As a yogi committed to growth, you, too, will have these breakthroughs on your way to greatness. What I've learned, and what I teach about Savasana, is don't wait until you find yourself in these dark times to find the higher purpose of your life.

Savasana is an opportunity to allow new things to be. Tapping into something greater for yourself begins with the awareness that something greater even exists—and to recognize it. In Savasana, you can tap into that expansiveness and allow yourself to envision (or inwardly inquire about) your higher purpose, and what you want to have as a real possibility.

Like peeling an onion, Savasana is a process of letting go layer by layer in a series of openings, which occur with increasing depth. When you release fully into Savasana, you get to look within and discover something profound about yourself. You come to know yourself—not what you think, not what you feel, not what you've accomplished, but who you are truthfully, at your essence.

You become yourself in the moment when all the ideas and concepts that you've been carrying around about yourself are dissolved in the light of your awareness. You come to the ultimate state of "nothingness," and from that fertile state, you become pure possibility. From that essence of you, you can then move into authentic, meaningful creation of your life. In other words, you get to pause, hit the reset button, and consciously choose your actions moving forward from a place of pure authenticity—no masks, no struggles, no doubt, no contraction. You can ask yourself, *What am I truly a yes for? What do I want to create?* You move from being passively curious to passionately interested in the direction of your life and your practice.

In Savasana, you can allow yourself to experience what you want in the future right here and now. Inner vision becomes clear as the drishti in your heart opens and sees. You will become more directed and more focused as you look and listen from your heart. When the head wants something, it will never go directly; it will zigzag, or spin in a whirlpool as it considers pros and cons, pathways and obstacles. But the whisperings from the heart are always authentic and singular in their focus. The heart knows what it wants.

The problems, challenges, and issues that most of us have now in our practice and our lives will be resolved only when we come back to knowing ourselves as a visionary from the heart. Each of us must come to the realization that we can practice and live at the level of Executive Creator of our own lives, in concert with a force greater than ourselves, rather than following an inherited or imagined vision of ourselves that we may have adopted from what has historically been expected of us.

Savasana offers the experience of opening your heart to hear its wisdom. It is an opportunity to know and be yourself—unfiltered, unencumbered, and unburdened. This deeply satisfying experience of yourself, as yourself, is a sign that your practice is working.

•

Acknowledge yourself for bringing yourself to your mat today. That's your commitment in action. What do you appreciate about how you showed up, what you accomplished? Appreciation is a recognition of the contribution you've made. This is how we cultivate a grateful and happy heart.

As well, acknowledge where you got stopped in your practice, where you maybe didn't accomplish what you wanted to today, knowing you will have the opportunity to refine next time. Acknowledgment is the acceptance of truth and allows something to be whole and complete as it is. Honor yourself by being honest. This is the practice of *satya*. Where did you hold back? When did you choose fear? Where did you avoid being uncomfortable or shrink away from your edge? What was your contribution to whatever it is you are concerned with in your practice? These questions are an antidote to any feelings of helplessness and, by affirming that we had a role in creating our experience, allow us to choose accountability. Just acknowledge the answers; that's where the power lies. It's not a failing on your part. No blame, no fault— just awareness. It's actually a win to become conscious of where you got stopped, because then it becomes a foundation for growth.

Every fact carries the weight of the meaning you give it. If you view the points you held back as a failing, you'll hold it as that. But if you view it as simply one opportunity you didn't take, you can choose to do it differently the next time. Don't waste time being disappointed in yourself; that's a dead end. The famous radio host Bernard Meltzer wisely once said, "When you forgive, you in no way change the past—but you sure do change the future."

I find it helpful to remember, as I step off my yoga mat and onto the mat called my life, that through today's practice I reframed the whole context of my life. As I lift my body up from Savasana, I remind myself I now have the power to see everything that comes my way in life as a pose. In the stance of true north, I now have the power, stability, freedom, flexibility, and openness to keep things simple and live from the heart: singular in purpose, straightforward, and upset free.

Standing in the space of what you've accomplished and not accomplished, what is the future you're now creating for yourself and your practice? Where do you go from here? The accomplishments are done . . . remember, today's breakthrough is tomorrow's ego trip. Enjoy them, fill your heart with gratitude in this moment, and then let them go. Keep the space clear for new insights, discoveries, and breakthroughs. Same for the places where you got stopped. Acknowledge them, let them go, and look to what you're now creating from here.

As always, the question to ask ourselves is *What's now possible?*

acknowledgments

I have deep appreciation for the many people who saw me through the creation of this book:

The brilliant work and collaboration of Debra Goldstein, who provided immense insight, listened, and fully supported the final outcome of this book.

Everyone at Hay House, especially Reid Tracy and Sally Mason, for empowering and enabling me to publish this book.

Ned Leavitt, my literary agent, who supported and encouraged me every step of the way with patience and love.

Erin Anderson, for her talented cover design.

Pauline Caballero and the rest of the amazing Baptiste Institute team, who supported me through the process of writing this book, in spite of all the time it took me away from the other incredible work of the Baptiste Institute.

The multitude of leaders, teachers, and affiliated studios who are so powerfully carrying forth the message of Baptiste Yoga by creating communities of great people all over the planet.

I am grateful to every participant who has ever attended a program, workshop, or training with me. Your willingness to listen, do the work, and grow is what makes this journey of teaching extraordinary for me.

Last but not least, I thank my family: my parents, Walt and Magana Baptiste, have been wholeheartedly committed to living lives that make a real contribution to others and have shown me the way. My three beautiful sons—Luke, Jacob, and Malachi—are three extraordinary young men committed to living extraordinary lives.

about the author

For more than 25 years, Baron Baptiste has devoted his life to creating and sharing transformational yoga practices and programs. He shares the Baptiste Yoga methodology through workshops, books, yoga teacher trainings, and his continued work with non-profit organizations.

A social entrepreneur and visionary, Baron is committed to sharing Baptiste Yoga in ways that make a real and lasting difference in the lives of people across the planet. His approach to yoga has been a catalyst for society's acceptance of yoga as a popular practice and is now being used by millions of people globally.

Website: www.baptisteyoga.com

resources

About the Baptiste Institute

Baptiste Institute is an organization changing lives by bringing yoga to the world as a leadership skill. We inspire people to fulfill their purpose of making a difference for themselves and others, teaching yoga as a path of transformation to a healthier, happier, and more powerful life. We develop and design our products, programs, and classes so they are relevant to your every waking moment and accessible for all levels of abilities, ages, and interests.

Continue your journey into the art and soul of yoga practice and explore some of the many tools for transformation we offer.

Online Offerings

Our video and audio products, books, and podcasts are an easy way for you to explore the transformational process at home or on the road. Additionally, we offer a wide range of yoga clothing to enhance your practice.

Visit www.baptisteyoga.com or call 1-800-936-9642 for the latest product offerings.

Program Offerings

If you are ready to take a bold step in your life and enter the flow at a totally different angle, consider one of our programs. We offer programs that range from one day to one week for those aspiring to expand their practice or their teaching.

Baptiste Institute's programs are an exclusive hands-on opportunity to hone your practice on and off the mat. Aspiring teachers will be empowered to transform the lives of others seeking physical and spiritual growth, leading them to a healthier state of existence. We establish a unique learning environment in which you can challenge yourself like never before. You won't just learn skills *intellectually*—you will put them into practice immediately, achieving incredible results that will stay with you forever. Attend one of our programs and you will learn more, do more, achieve more, and grow more than you could ever imagine.

Visit www.baptisteyoga.com or call 1-800-936-9642 for the latest program offerings.

Baptiste Yoga Partner Studios

Our partner studios offer all-levels classes for students of different levels of experience and fitness abilities. We teach a practice with a solid physical base coupled with an intellectual understanding in which to continue your journey into power. Attending classes at our partner studios will expand your peace of mind and vitality of spirit while helping you build strength, stamina, flexibility, and encourage an overall renewed personal force.

Visit www.baptisteyoga.com or call 1-800-936-9642 for studio locations.

Baptiste Foundation

Baptiste Foundation is a non-profit organization contributing to individuals and communities in need by sharing the powerful tools and techniques of Baptiste Yoga. When the timeless principles of Baptiste Yoga are practiced, we believe that our struggles can be transcended, bringing light to darkness. Baptiste Yoga is practiced by everyone across the world and from all walks of life: CEOs, professional athletes, recovering addicts, Wounded Warriors, veterans with PTSD and more, all with similar results that include inner peace, sparked inspiration in purpose, and the creation of new possibilities in every realm of life.

Visit www.baptistefoundation.org to get involved, contribute, and for more information.

For more information on Baron check out baronbaptiste.com or follow him on Instagram: @baronbaptisteyoga.

Stay Connected With Us

**Follow and engage with our
community on social media:**

Facebook: www.facebook.com/baptisteyoga
Twitter: www.twitter.com/baptisteyoga
Instagram: www.instagram.com/baptisteyoga
YouTube: www.youtube.com/baptisteyoga

Hay House Titles of Related Interest

YOU CAN HEAL YOUR LIFE, the movie,
starring Louise Hay & Friends
(available as a 1-DVD program
and an expanded 2-DVD set)
Watch the trailer at: www.LouiseHayMovie.com

THE SHIFT, the movie,
starring Dr. Wayne W. Dyer
(available as a 1-DVD program
and an expanded 2-DVD set)
Watch the trailer at: www.DyerMovie.com

•

LIFE LOVES YOU: 7 Spiritual Practices to Heal Your Life,
by Louise Hay and Robert Holden

MIRACLES NOW: 108 Life-Changing Tools for Less Stress, More Flow, and Finding Your True Purpose, by Gabrielle Bernstein

THE TRUE SOURCE OF HEALING: How the Ancient Tibetan Practice of Soul Retrieval Can Transform and Enrich Your Life, by Tenzin Wangyal Rinpoche

WHY MEDITATE: Working with Thoughts and Emotions, by Matthieu Ricard

All of the above are available at your local bookstore,
or may be ordered by contacting Hay House (see next page).

•

We hope you enjoyed this Hay House book. If you'd like to receive our online catalog featuring additional information on Hay House books and products, or if you'd like to find out more about the Hay Foundation, please contact:

Hay House, Inc., P.O. Box 5100, Carlsbad, CA 92018-5100
(760) 431-7695 or (800) 654-5126
(760) 431-6948 (fax) or (800) 650-5115 (fax)
www.hayhouse.com® • www.hayfoundation.org

•

Published and distributed in Australia by:
Hay House Australia Pty. Ltd., 18/36 Ralph St., Alexandria NSW 2015
Phone: 612-9669-4299 • *Fax:* 612-9669-4144 • www.hayhouse.com.au

Published and distributed in the United Kingdom by: Hay House UK, Ltd.,
Astley House, 33 Notting Hill Gate, London W11 3JQ
Phone: 44-20-3675-2450 • *Fax:* 44-20-3675-2451 • www.hayhouse.co.uk

Published and distributed in the Republic of South Africa by:
Hay House SA (Pty), Ltd., P.O. Box 990, Witkoppen 2068
info@hayhouse.co.za • www.hayhouse.co.za

Published in India by: Hay House Publishers India,
Muskaan Complex, Plot No. 3, B-2, Vasant Kunj, New Delhi 110 070
Phone: 91-11-4176-1620 • *Fax:* 91-11-4176-1630 • www.hayhouse.co.in

Distributed in Canada by: Raincoast Books,
2440 Viking Way, Richmond, B.C. V6V 1N2 •
Phone: 1-800-663-5714 • *Fax:* 1-800-565-3770 • www.raincoast.com

•

Take Your Soul on a Vacation

Visit www.HealYourLife.com® to regroup, recharge, and reconnect with your own magnificence. Featuring blogs, mind-body-spirit news, and life-changing wisdom from Louise Hay and friends.

Visit www.HealYourLife.com today!

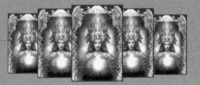